THE BEST WOMEN'S MONOLOGUES FROM NEW PLAYS, 2019

THE BEST WOMEN'S MONOLOGUES FROM NEW PLAYS, 2019

EDITED AND WITH AN INTRODUCTION BY
LAWRENCE HARBISON

APPLAUSE
THEATRE & CINEMA BOOKS
Guilford, Connecticut

Published by Applause Theatre & Cinema Books
An imprint of The Rowman & Littlefield Publishing Group, Inc.
4501 Forbes Blvd., Ste. 200
Lanham, MD 20706
www.rowman.com

Distributed by NATIONAL BOOK NETWORK

British Library Cataloguing in Publication Information Available

Library of Congress Cataloging-in-Publication Data Available

ISBN 978-1-4930-5331-5 (pbk. : alk. paper)
ISBN 978-1-4930-5332-2 (electronic)

♾️™ The paper used in this publication meets the minimum requirements of American National Standard for Information Sciences—Permanence of Paper for Printed Library Materials, ANSI/NISO Z39.48-1992.

CONTENTS

INTRODUCTION

Here you will find a rich and varied selection of monologues for women, most of which are from plays of recent vintage, many of them produced and/or published in the 2018–2019 theatrical season. Many are for younger performers (teens through 30s), but there are also some excellent pieces for older women as well. The age of the character is indicated in each monologue, but you will find that many may be done by actors of different ages. Some are comic (laughs), some are dramatic (generally, no laughs), some are seriocomic (some laughs). Some are rather short and some are rather long. All represent the best in contemporary playwriting.

Several of the monologues are by playwrights whose work may be familiar to you, such as Don Nigro, Theresa Rebeck, Arleen Hutton, Constance Condon, Richard Vetere, Sam Bobrick, and Sharr White (whom I interviewed for my book, *How I Did It: Establishing a Playwriting Career* [Applause Theatre & Cinema Books]); others are by exciting up-and-comers such as Boni B. Alvarez, Chiara Atik, Fengar Gael, Jessica Lind Peterson, Daniel Damiano, Christopher Demos-Brown, Jacqueline Goldfinger, Suzanne Bradbeer, Kate Scelsa, Reina Hardy, Nandita Shenoy, and Sam Chanse. Many of the plays from which these monologues have been culled have been published, and hence are readily available either from the publisher/licensor or from a theatrical book store such as the Drama Book Shop in New York. Some may not be published for a while, in which case you may contact the author or agent to request a copy of the entire text of the play containing the monologue that suits your fancy. Information on publishers/rights holders may be found in the Rights and Permissions section in the back of this anthology.

Break a leg in that audition! Knock 'em dead in class!

Lawrence Harbison

P.S. Although each monologue lists the character's age, many would work perfectly well for an actor of a different age.

ACCORDING TO THE CHORUS
Arlene Hutton

Seriocomic
AUDREY, could be any age

In the basement quick-change area of a long-running Broadway production, AUDREY is training KJ, the new dresser. It's a half hour before curtain.

AUDREY   Nicki comes off downstage left, just as the train's going past. It's not like a real train piece, it's a plywood front, but the stagehands move it, so it's not at the same place every night, depending on if we have the regular crew or subs. You're at the edge of the proscenium—you know what that is, right?—just off stage. She comes to you, you don't go to her, 'cause if you did you'd be seen by the audience, right? So you're standing there and she comes to you. Watch me. The hat is on your head, purse on your right arm, dress unzipped and on your arms like this, so your hands are through it. See? Nicki comes offstage and turns her back to you. It's one, unzip the dress she has on. Two, pull it off her shoulders and let it drop to the floor. Three, new dress over her head. Four, pull dress down. Five, zip dress, six, hat on her head, then, hand her the purse and she's on stage. You've got seven seconds for the change. While the train is going by. The chorus girls have the fastest changes, on deck, in the wings, but if there's time we change them down here in the basement. I've got Monica and Linda, they're a handful, Brenda dresses Joyce and Stacie, when she goes on, Stacie's the swing, and you'll be taking care of Jessica and Nicki. Nicki's new and she's the one with the seven second change in the wings. Okay, now.

[*She marks the change again, counting the beats, as if it were choreography, perhaps even snapping her fingers to the beat.*]

1

Unzip, drop. Over, pull down. Zip. Hat. Purse. You have to make certain you don't get the fabric stuck in the zipper. [*Pause.*] No one lasts in your position. I don't know why. Brenda and I have been here from the beginning, but your position has been a revolving door. Maybe you shouldn't have left the opera. Just because this show been running since way before *Cats* doesn't mean it's a sure thing. [*Pause.*] I'm joking. I'm gonna retire on this show. Oh, and speaking of running forever, watch out for Brenda. She's too old for all the stairs and she'll have you racing around doing her job, too, if you're not careful. And don't try to make friends with the chorus girls. You're here to change their costumes, not have social time. Okay, let's go upstairs. It's not half hour yet. I'll show you where you stand and you can practice it once in the dark.

AFTER

Michael McKeever

Dramatic
JULIA CAMPBELL, 40s–50s

JULIA CAMPBELL *discusses her son's three-day detention with her sister and explains why she has invited the mother of the boy who has accused him of bullying to her house.*

JULIA   I took his phone away. All three days. [*Beat.*] Don't look at me that way. I can be "Bitch-Mom" when I have to be. You should have been here three days ago when I took it from him. Now that was a show. I said to him, "*Do you want me to be like her? Do you want me to start going through your phone to see what's on it, being suspicious of everything you do?*" Of course, he was horrified. I said, "*Help me then. Help me to understand* why. Explain to me who this person is who sent this text. Because it *sure as hell* isn't the young man I raised. *We don't use words like that in this house.*" And he looks at me all defiant and say, "Don't we Mom? Don't we?" And then he shakes his head and walks away. Like I'm clueless. And you know what? *I am* clueless. I don't . . . *I don't understand him. I don't understand his world.* [*Beat.*] I try, I really do. *He's a good boy.* He's not a bully. He just . . . [*Beat.*] He has such potential. When I think of what he can be. And yet, the more I try to help him, the farther he pulls away. [*Beat, she looks off.*] She told Donna McNaughten that I was a bad mother. It seems, yesterday, Donna McNaughten ran into Connie at the bank. She asked her about Kyle's suspension and the text. Apparently, that's all everyone is talking about. And Connie told her the entire story in graphic detail. She had the nerve to tell her that all of this was a direct result of my substandard parenting. It seems I'm this terrible mother who has no control over her kid. That I'm more concerned about what I'm wearing or what my china pattern looks like—or some such bullshit—than the upbringing of my son. And, of course, fucking Donna McNaughten couldn't get home fast enough to share this with me. Connie Beckman is being a bitch and she needs to be called on it.

THE AFTERPARTY
Reina Hardy

Seriocomic
CLAIRE, 30s

CLAIRE LE VERRIER, *a poet haunted by the death of her childhood crush, is trying to compose a poem so beautiful that it will make a star step out of the sky. In this excerpt, she lectures the audience about love.*

CLAIRE   I knew a guy—it didn't work out—who always liked to ask people "What's your favorite story about love?" He said he found the answer very revealing, but I think he just wanted to tell people that his favorite was "The origin of love" from the Aristophanes section of the ***Symposium, which I think he thought made him an enlightened being . . . because it's all about equality . . . you know, in the iron-forge days of the earth every human was a big ball with four legs and two faces, until the gods got pissed and split us down the middle, and so we spend every waking moment trying to smash ourselves back together with our other halves? But Aristophanes was a comedian. His job was to make funny stories where everything works out ok. And while it's nice to think that we all have soulmates out there, we have to remember that there were scientists at that party too, and they came to a completely different conclusion, that didn't have much to do with equality, and had kind of a lot to do with banging your teacher. And honestly that makes sense to me. If you're going to run around trying to be a part of something . . . wouldn't you try to be a part of something bigger?

THE AFTERPARTY
Reina Hardy

Seriocomic
CLAIRE, 30s

CLAIRE LE VERRIER, *a poet haunted by the death of her childhood crush, is trying to compose a poem so beautiful that it will make a star step out of the sky. Here, she thinks about the universe as she prepares to deliver her poem.*

CLAIRE   So there's a general idea that poets are dippy and scientists are practical and hard edged. This . . . is . . . true . . . By and large. But here's another dopey thing some scientists say, and I mean people with doctorates who write books. We are the universe dreaming itself into consciousness. How high do you have to be to write that sentence down? This is the idea—we . . . we humans, with our clever little thumbs and monkey brains, are capable of understanding the universe. And because we are capable of it, it must be our job. Just as it is the job of the stars to cook our elements in their hearts, and to shine energy down on us through the cold night so that we can build telescopes and long-range radio satellites to send our prayers right back up. Doesn't all that sound awfully familiar to you? We spend centuries wandering in the desert, answering to an imaginary tribal lunatic just so that we can feel we are chosen snowflakes, and after we have sixty revolutions and a lot of people die, we haven't gotten over that feeling at all? Copernicus and Kepler and Galileo and Herschel went to all that trouble to knock us out of the center of the universe, and here we are again, sitting on our butts like the Buddha, contemplating that you-are-here dot. Of course, we are at the center of the observable universe. By definition. Also by definition. The observable universe is the only one we get.

AMERICA ADJACENT
Boni B. Alvarez

Dramatic
AIMEE, 35, Filipina

Seven months pregnant, AIMEE bides her time in a cramped Los Angeles birthing house so that her baby will be born an American citizen. Being with child, AIMEE's libido is in overdrive. Her husband, Rogelio, is back in the Philippines. Here, she shares with a fellow resident how much she misses sex.

AIMEE   I miss Rogelio's breath, how hot it is when he blow in my ear, and he is kissing my neck. To be under him, feeling his weight, all of his weight on me. I look at him, into his dark eyes. His eyes look so happy, like they are dancing, so excited that we are one. More hot breath, *ha?* Then his beautiful long eyelashes flutter, and his eyes will become sad. Sad, maybe because it will soon be over. And then when we are almost there, breathing hot together, he try to be quiet, not to scream, and it is as if he is crying. The cry of sex and his body, it shakes, shivering. When this happen, my body, my goodness, it feels as if I am filled with sweetness, an ocean of candies flooding inside me. Wave after wave and more waves. We are quiet, but breathing loud . . . and then we laugh. We laugh! He pulls me close, keeping me warm, holding me tight with hands, his arms, his legs, his body making me safe. It is not only sex . . . it is love also.

AMERICA ADJACENT
Boni B. *Alvarez*

Dramatic
SAMPAGUITA, 20, Filipina

SAMPAGUITA *has traveled from the Philippines, biding her time in a cramped Los Angeles birthing house so her baby will be born an American citizen. The reality of hiding in the United States illegally has tarnished her image of the American Dream. Here, she speaks to her unborn son.*

SAMPAGUITA   *Aray,* Lorenzo. I know you are tired. I am tired also, but I cannot sleep if you will continue kicking so much. You rest your feet, *ha?*

[*She rubs her belly.*]

I know you don't like it here. [*Beat.*] I don't want to be here either. I am sorry. But your Lolo make a big sacrifice for us to come here. He spend a lot of money.

[*She sits.*]

I am your Mama. You must listen to me. [*Beat.*] I will not know everything, *ha?* I tell you this now, so you must be understanding. Patient. And forgiving. [*Beat.*] When you are older, I will let you choose. Not like me, no choice really. You will decide, Lorenzo. You can stay in Bacolod, continue with your Lolo's farming. You can go to Manila if you want to be a city boy. Do your schooling there if you like.

[*She rubs her belly.*]

You can travel. Tokyo, Dubai, London. With your passport, you will be a guest of the world. [*Pause.*] If you want to return here . . . you can start a business making *lumpia.* You can sell *lumpia* from a truck. Maybe you will marry a

Hollywood *artista*, live in a house with a jacuzzi. [*Neat.*] You can be President of this country, Lorenzo [*Beat.*] You qualify. [*Pause.*] You are an American. Everything is for your consideration.

AMERICAN SON
Christopher Demos-Brown

Dramatic
KENDRA, 40s–early 50s, African American

KENDRA *is waiting with her estranged husband,* SCOTT *(who is White), at a police station very late at night. Their son, Jamal, a high school senior, went out with some friends but never returned home, and* KENDRA *and* SCOTT *are waiting impatiently as the police try to figure out if anything has happened to him. Last summer, Jamal wanted to re-create Sherman's March to the Sea in reverse with a White friend, but his parents wouldn't let him.* SCOTT *felt he was too young.*

KENDRA   "Too young"? "Too young" had nothing to do with it. (Shit), my granddaddy was fighting in Okinawa when he was seventeen. ("Too young"). It wasn't that. It was the prospect of him driving through the Deep South . . . my son alone with a White boy driving Sherman's March to the Sea in reverse. Maybe he and Jeff stop at a gas station in some little town . . . 'Cause he doesn't know any better. 'Cause we raised him to believe the world's full of goodness. And he starts batting his doe eyes at some cute l'il White girl. Maybe the two of 'em walk into a burger joint happens to be an "alt right" hangout. Maybe some guy with a swastika tattooed on his biceps had a little too much to drink . . . doesn't like the look of this boy who's poisoning the country's racial purity. [*Beat.*] But the worst one . . . the one that always comes back . . . is I see him getting stopped by a cop for doing nothing in particular. I see ankle-high boots and badges and nightsticks. And I think back on that night when I was five years old and watched my stoic mother doubled over sobbing in the kitchen 'cause Arthur McDuffie'd been beaten to death by the cops . . . and they'd acquitted those cops. [*Beat.*] And you were a l'il boy asleep on the other side of town dreaming of becoming one.

[*Beat.*]

I'm scared.

THE ANTELOPE PARTY
Eric John Meyer

Seriocomic
MAGGIE, early to mid-20s

MAGGIE *is sharing a nighttime walk home with a friend who definitely has a crush on her. She's recently been through a strange, difficult experience, and her friend just asked her about what happened. It was frightening and crazy, but since it involves her family, she's trying to put a positive spin on it—for her friend as well as for herself.* MAGGIE *is a Brony. Bronies are adult fans of the children's cartoon* My Little Pony.

MAGGIE   When they called me over, Doug was like "you don't need to talk to those Neighborhood Watch douche bags" but I saw my cousin with them in the car and I hadn't seen him since he left for Atlanta like four years ago. So I went over and the first thing he says is "What are you doing with all that shit on your head?" I told him I was enjoying myself and that he should try it sometime. And that's when he grabbed me and pulled me into the car. And I was like "What the fuck? Where are you taking me?" and he says he's taking me to see my dad. That my dad was going to make me rethink what I wore out on the street. He's so full of shit. No one did much talking in the car. Even when we stopped for the pizza. Then my phone rang and one of them said "Who's that, your boyfriend?" I said I didn't have one. And then my cousin was like "That's because all the guys you hang out with are fags." I tried to argue, but they didn't want to hear it. I thought for sure they'd take my phone away if I answered it, so I didn't pick up. They took me to his house. He was just sitting there at the kitchen table waiting for me. He looked older in a way that made him handsome, and . . . he was taller. He had a nice shirt on. A fresh haircut. I thought, "who is this man and what is he doing with this bunch of redneck losers?" And just then—like, right then—he said "I know what you're thinking. I know what people think of us. But I want you to hear about it from me." Like, it should have been weird, but it didn't feel weird. I took my wig off as soon as I walked in, but he said he wasn't mad at me. He just wanted me to be safe. I told him I was—that you all were my friends. And he said that he'd heard some things about kids around town, so he wanted to make sure—that that's what family is for and that's what the Neighborhood Watch is for. And that people didn't understand them sometimes, but what they did was never bad. Like how people were always suspicious of Batman and Superman because nobody knew who they were. He said the Neighborhood Watch was the same way. They had to do things in secret, but street crime was down by half since they started. And lots of people were glad they were there, even if they couldn't say so in public. It felt good to see him, and so proud of himself. And to see how much he wanted my approval for what he was doing. I thought: this is what The Show teaches us. This is what being a Pony is all about: giving this man the love of his daughter. So I hugged him and took the secret pledge and after that everyone eased up and we ate pizza and I heard all about how Atlanta didn't work out for my cousin and how he was back now looking for work in Pittsburgh. It made my dad happy. Besides, I figured maybe I can bring a little Brony Tolerance and Love to the Neighborhood Watch.

ANYWHERE
Michael Ross Albert

Dramatic
JOY, late 20s–early 30s

JOY *is a struggling single mom who rents out her basement through Airbnb to help raise money for her terminally ill son. After her newest guest, LIZ—a businesswoman in town for a conference—has stayed for a few days, the two women spend a night partying together, along with JOY's recalcitrant boyfriend. The night of heavy drinking leads to an unnerving encounter that LIZ can't quite remember the next day. As she prepares to leave the suburban household, JOY makes a desperate attempt to solidify their connection, revealing more sinister motivations.*

JOY   I'm sorry you feel like this didn't mean anything. Because it did to me. [*Pause.*] This morning, before he went back to his apartment, Kyle said he thought we should move in together. We've been (well I guess he told you about this) we're taking a sort of a break. I need to be focused on my son, and his treatment, and with Kyle, it can sometimes feel like I have two little boys to look after. He's never been married before. Surprise surprise. And he has a tendency to be a really shitty influence on me. If Ethan's staying at my ex's and I don't have a rental downstairs, his friends come over and stay up all night, and I spend the next day airing out the smell of smoke. But, he's got this security job at the bank now, which seems to be going great. He's almost done the probation period and he hasn't missed a single day yet. And last night, I don't know what you said to him, but . . . You inspired him. He said you gave him this great advice and that he was going to commit himself to me, and to Ethan. And I actually believe him. Oh shit, listen to me. I'm officially drunk. Sorry to ramble on like this. Whatever it was you said: You changed

14

our lives. It didn't mean nothing, you staying here. Kyle and I might really make it through this, you know, whatever it is. Obstacle course. Battlefield. You name it. [*Small beat.*] Of course, there is a catch, though. A fly in the ointment. Nothing serious. It's just, Kyle's apartment is always in one disaster situation or another. And the landlord is a complete scumbag. Kyle wants to break his rental agreement so he can move in here, but he's still got four months left on the lease. The truth is, it's not a great building. There's always something wrong with the unit. He's not gonna find someone crazy enough to pay eighteen hundred dollars a month to live there. If he were to move out now, he'd be stuck with paying the rent for the next four months. That's, like, more than seven thousand dollars. And if he doesn't pay, the landlord'll probably take him to court. He's that kind of person.

ANYWHERE
Michael Ross Albert

Dramatic
LIZ, late 20s–early 30s

JOY *is a struggling single mom who rents out her basement through Airbnb to help raise money for her terminally ill son. After her newest guest,* LIZ—*a businesswoman in town for a conference—has stayed for a few days, the two women spend a night partying together, along with* JOY's *recalcitrant boyfriend. The night of heavy drinking leads to an unnerving encounter that* LIZ *can't quite remember the next day. As she prepares to leave the suburban household,* JOY *makes a desperate attempt to solidify their connection, revealing more sinister motivations. When* JOY *reveals she intends to blackmail* LIZ *by sending a video from the previous night to* LIZ's *husband,* LIZ *refuses to pay.*

LIZ   Is this your first time blackmailing someone? Don't you know, you never let the customer name their own price? That's a terrible bargaining tactic. First you say, "Give me seven thousand dollars and I won't send this video to your husband." I say, "Nah, that's too rich for my blood; I think I'll work things out with Richard on my own." Then, traditionally, you would say something like, "Okay, I'll go easy on you. Five thousand dollars." And I would probably say something like, "You know, it's not really a great time for me to be blackmailed right now? We're saving up for that one vacation we've never had the chance to take since our honeymoon and money's really tight." And then you say, "Alright. Since you're a nice person, I'm gonna cut you a deal. Thirty-five hundred, and a bottle of vodka, to make up for what you and Kyle and I drank last night. That's more than fair, don't you think?" And I would say, "I dunno, Joy, that still sounds pretty steep to me. If I'd known you'd want me to reimburse you for the booze, I certainly wouldn't have shared a drink with you in the first place." And then you'd say, "Two thousand. I'm practically giving this away. Isn't your marriage worth a measly two grand? That's practically nothing to you and your husband, but do you know what a difference two thousand dollars could do for me and my sick, sick fucking son?" And by this point, I'd see how desperate you were. How pathetic and how sad, and how stupid you are for thinking you could get away with this, for even trying to intimidate me. For drugging me last night—And planning all this with your dirtbag of a boyfriend who, I guarantee you, will not be your boyfriend for long.

APES AT PLAY
Jonathan Yukich

Seriocomic
AGENT BLUE, 40s–50s

AGENT BLUE *reflects on a moment of intimacy that led to her becoming a hired killer.*

BLUE   Did you know the Statue of Liberty's head isn't centered? It's off by two feet. People gawked at her for decades, without ever noticing. It's astonishing what we miss, even when looking right at a thing. I've been to the top, you know. I had sex in the crown. Sorry. Too much? It's closed now, of course—the crown. Not because of anything I did, I assure you. The boy and I were looking out over the harbor. We started necking. Things got frisky. There was intercourse. Fumbling and unsatisfying, but still intercourse. No one even noticed. We were in a blanket, tightly wrapped. And all I kept thinking, as he awkwardly stabbed at me from behind, is what an ideal spot this would be for a sniper. You can see the entire harbor, and no one can see you. Clear shot. It's at that moment that I knew what I was to do with my life. I would become an assassin. A killer in the shadows. When it was over, the boy bought me a Popsicle, and told me he was in love. Can you imagine? I don't recall his name, but the Popsicle was grape.

BABEL
Jacqueline Goldfinger
Dramatic
RENEE, 30s

RENEE is talking to her female partner, DANI, about possibly aborting their fetus during the first weeks of pregnancy because the doctor's prenatal tests show that the resulting child could be severely disfigured. In this futuristic world, children have to pass a certification test to guarantee they have good genetics or they are segregated from the full community.

RENEE   There are things, aberrations, long lines of . . . He showed me the graph and there were these spikes of, misgivings? They indicate, could indicate, might indicate, sociopathy. Or extreme anger. There's no way to actually know what nurture, how it will change the, or not change, the, the baby. The child. There would be genetic re-testing at age 18. But he wanted us to think about, even with the unknown-ingness of it all. He highly recommended. That we take the shot. That we, end the pregnancy. One quick shot. An hour waiting in his office. Maybe a few cramps. And then, we can begin again. Immediately. He recommended, because these test results. These signs, signs and wonders of modern medicine, okay? With these test results, no one would issue a PRE certificate. The baby would be . . . Uncertified. Uncertifiable. Possibly never certified. Possibly, with long term observation and hundreds of thousands of dollars in carers and early intervention specialists and everything else, possibly certified. Tested again at 18. Maybe certified. And if not, Stuck. Being, One of Them, Forced into a life of, monitoring and manual labor and . . . Or, or take the shot. Now. And we begin again. Now would be the best time, he said.

BABEL

Jacqueline Goldfinger

Dramatic
RENEE, 30s

RENEE *is talking to her female partner,* DANI, *about voting for a law governing genetic testing that she is unsure about.*

RENEE   I keep seeing it. The button. Just, staring at it. All that time, queuing to vote. And I couldn't vote for it. And I couldn't vote against it. I just didn't vote. And now, I may have doomed our baby. To a life among the rejects, in the ghettos. And who can only rise to, are only permitted certain jobs, certain lives. And us, blamed by, friends, family. By us. And I look at our life. And what we've made out of our shabby genetic materials. If our parents had . . . If they would have known about what was possible, The worst that was possible in us, for us, as children, as adults, If they would have known the full range of our possible dysfunction? But if you know the worst of what someone is capable of, can you ever really love them, for the best in themselves? Or do you just live in fear of what they are capable of? And do you inadvertently teach them to fear what they have locked inside, even if it's not who they truly are? I don't want to raise a child in fear. I think I felt a little like God that day. That day I was looking at the button. With you waiting outside, mumbling about breakfast. I think I liked it. The shining promise of controlling, the uncontrollable. The power of, I think I liked it. Or the idea of it, at least. And that's why it was so hard to make a decision. Because, logically, and in my heart, I knew that voting for these tests was wrong, but Jesus H. Fucking Christ on a stick did it feel good to have the power of God, damn the consequences. And they made it so easy to push the button. To be God.

BAILEY'S COLLEGE FUND

James Hindman

COMIC
VERA, 40s–60s

*A devoted mother and wife, VERA has spent her life doing every-
thing by the books. Now, with her kids out of the house and a new
baby in her life, VERA is making her own rules! This monologue is
addressed directly to the audience.*

VERA   Just when I'd gotten the last one off to college and out of
the house—lo and behold—a new baby! And he is the light
of my life! He'll be nine next month. I carry him in a pouch on
my belly. He only weighs four and a half pounds. He's a York-
shire terrier! A rescue from the ASPCA. And I love him madly.
His name is George Bailey. I was a big Jimmy Stewart fan. I
am offended how some people refuse to accept that Bailey's
my child just because he isn't human. Who says that your
children have to be the same species? You should meet my
other kids. Human? With the pierced tongue and the blue
hair . . . who can tell? I saw on Sixty Minutes, this pig saved
a baby's life. Jumped in the pond, pulled it out and licked it
dry. Like it was its own child. That is a motherly instinct. They
showed a chicken raising a gerbil, a whale raising a dolphin,
a lion raising a bear! When are we humans going to figure
it out? Look around . . . what do you see? People fighting.
Ripping each other apart. You want world peace? Raise a
giraffe. Bring a tiger into your nest and sit on 'em. We are all
God's creatures! Not to mention the health benefits. When
I got Bailey, my blood pressure went down. I don't need my
medication. I sleep better. I'm happier. That's why I've started
. . . and not a word of this to my husband. I've started up a
college fund at work. Twenty-five dollars a week. Nobody
knows it's for Obedience School. Including the IRS. That's

right—I'm taking Bailey's college fund as a tax deduction. I'll have two at Texas Tech and one at Kathy Cooper's Canine Campus. Little Bailey's gonna be jumpin' and sittin' and rollin' over—and I'm gonna treat him like a king for doing it.

[*She starts to exit, then has a second thought.*]

Oh! . . . Oh! . . . Last week I had the flu. Couldn't move out of bed. Three grown kids—Not *one* of them came to my room to visit. But my Bailey? That dog sat right there at the foot of my bed, every day, licking my feet. Unconditional love. What more could a mother ask for in a child?

THE BANANA WAR
Arnold Johnston and Deborah Ann Percy
Dramatic
JOSÉFINA, 30s–50s

JOSÉFINA *is a member of a revolutionary group in a small, un-named Caribbean country. Here, she is speaking to* LUCY HAMIL-TON, *an American tourist, whom the group has kidnapped. The revolutionaries are using* LUCY *as a bargaining chip in their attempt to win concessions from the United States.*

JOSÉFINA   If you were a more important personage, Mrs. Hamilton, the United States government might mount some kind of rescue mission. If you were an undersecretary of state or the wife of someone important. But you are not. We have checked. You are the wife of a lawyer who hardly even practices law, who spends most of his time teaching at a university. As it is, there will be much press coverage. This will make your life meaningful. What meaning does it have now? You live in a safe brick house in the suburbs with three bathrooms, a basketball hoop over the garage door, and a hot tub in the back yard. Tomorrow you will be on the front page of *The New York Times*, *The Washington Post*, and *The Chicago Tribune*. Your life will take on more meaning than playing Lady Bountiful to a roomful of students. [*Beat.*] They will gather behind Mr. Hamilton, blonde, good-looking, con-cerned, sad-eyed. They will get the attention of middle-class America as no one else could. They will get the attention and sympathy of the French and the Germans and the English as no middle-class white man could. [*Beat.*] You will spend your vacation in a jail cell that is a palace by our standards. You will read *The New York Times* to pass the hours. Then you will go home with a story to tell.

BERNHARDT/HAMLET
Theresa Rebeck

Dramatic
SARAH BERNHARDT, 55

SARAH BERNHARDT, *the greatest actress of her time, is in rehears-als for a production of* Hamlet—*with her in the title role. Her lover, the playwright* EDMOND ROSTAND, *has warned her that the vultures are circling. This is her response.*

SARAH   I heed no warnings. If I had heeded any warning in my whole life, I'd have done nothing with it. I want no warnings! [*Beat.*] I'm sorry. I can't hear doubt right now, I'm swimming in it. Of course, of course this is who Hamlet is, the uncertainty, the relentlessness of it—especially in rehearsal going over and over, all that inaction, it's worse than a bore, and then of course there he is, the ghost of your father! His murderous rage, come from where? Where is it that fathers go? Not to the afterworld. No. I'm not afraid of death, nor is Hamlet, honestly, he's afraid merely of the night, the panic of the soul, the terrifying dread of meaninglessness. Gone in the light of day, but at night it is nothing but the most malicious of battles, sanity is at risk, at night and that is finally where Hamlet puts himself. Turning a saint into a murderer is no mean trick.

[*Angry now.*]

What was I supposed to do? Take a final bow, as Camille, silent, charming, graceful. And then exit stage left. Farewell, farewell. Or dwindle into the benevolent Gertrude? That's a trick question, don't answer it. How many times wafting through this play as Ophelia. Hamlet is Shakespeare himself, you know he is. It is why every actor hungers after him, finally, because we are convinced this is how you know him, soul to soul, but within this web of words what if he is nothing but annihilation? If they demean it. If they demean me. I can't. Honestly I can't even . . . please, go. You cannot stay if you merely come here to frighten me. I'm already out of my wits!

BIG SCARY ANIMALS
Matt Lyle

Comic
SOPHIA, 19–20, African American

SOPHIA's two dads are hosting their older, conservative, straight neighbors. Just when it seems the evening will pass without serious incident, SOPHIA enters and passionately starts oversharing with everyone in the room.

SOPHIA   So, Chase, like anyone has ever had a good relationship with a guy named Chase— We're at the movies, we've been "dating" for, what, a month, we've probably slept together fifty times at least, and this dude shows me his new— and mind you this is just as the movie is starting—he rolls up his sleeve, "Huh, huh, look," and shows me that he got an Iron Man tattoo. Iron Man. Fucking Iron Man. It hits me that I am dating a dude named after a bank who got an Iron Man tattoo. So, I asked him, "Why would you do that to your body?" He said, "Iron Man is cool." I'm like, "Grow a fucking goatee then. Don't permanently scar your body with a cartoon character. I beg of you, I say, you are too intelligent, I know your spirit is too deep to spend the rest of your life with everyone who sees your left arm thinking you must have gotten a tattoo when you were five years old. He's like, "Uhhh" and I'm like, "All you have to say is Uhh? How is our generation going to EVER be taken seriously if we are obsessed with some adolescent gun porn fantasy? What is it about guys and guns?! This dude's whole fucking body is a gun and he's your hero? Hero. Bullfuckingshit. You think Iron Man is a hero? Try Malala Yousafzai. What she stands in the face of would make Iron Man's dick crawl back inside his body and try to make an escape out of his butt." You know what I mean? Then he got up, said, "I'm breaking up with you," and left. And then the whole theater applauded for some reason.

BIRDS OF A FEATHER: A COMEDY ABOUT DE-EXTINCTION

June Guralnick

Comic

DIANA KATHERINE BIRDWHISTLE, nom de plume "Kate Bird," 20s

AP WELLS, a time-travelling scientist, has journeyed back to 1912 to save the passenger pigeon. He meets the play's heroine, DIANA KATHERINE BIRDWHISTLE, a fashionable member of high society, who has taken on the feather trade to stop the slaughter of birds. DIANA and AP have retreated to a park bench, discussing their morning undercover escapade.

DIANA   Your excessive description of the mating habits of birds of prey tipped off the feather trader that we were not hat buyers from Macy's! Mr. Wells, your scientific glass slides could not have captured today's horrible sight: thousands of birds—woodpeckers, robins, meadow-larks, warblers—murdered, their corpses dangling by ropes for buyers' inspection and purchase. My set would be shocked to learn of the wholesale destruction that ends in feathers perched on top of their hats. "What the ladies want, the ladies get," the trader said. But should the entirety of blame rest on the heads of the weaker sex? I grant women are gullible in desiring what we see in magazines, but is not what we see determined by men and their greed?

[Pointing to passers-by.]

There is Mrs. Van Cortland, in an absolute tizzy as revealed by her stiffly glazed straw hat sporting two owls, the head of a beaver, and feathers of an egret. Last week, she caught her husband in a compromising position—a fellow from his club. By the boathouse I spy Adelaide Van de Meer with Robert Brewster. Her most recent conquest is getting up the nerve to propose. The lady's coquettish cloche, a swirl of peacock feathers and wings of hummingbirds, indicates she is leaning in an affirmative direction both to Mr. Brewster's proposal and his fifteen million-a-year iron business . . . . However, make no mistake, Mr. Wells—I am no bird for your sport! By the age of six, I had read and committed to memory the classical works of Plato, Seneca, Confucius and the Words of the Buddha in the original Greek, Latin, Chinese and Sanskrit. By nine, I hid my intellect under school girl pinafores while consuming two thousand years of mathematical theories. By the age of 16 and my entry into society—in a lovely white chiffon dress with mauve and silver trim—I could recite, verbatim, treatises written by leading thinkers of our time: Darwin, Curie, Nietzsche, Freud, Einstein, even Bateson, an obscure scientist calling himself a geneticist. And today? My mind awakens each morning pulsating with dozens—no, hundreds—of ideas about science, philosophy and fashion! Ergo sum and in pointed summation, Mr. Wells—a century from now, unfettered by societal obligations and family expectations, you will find me journeying to stars not yet discovered by our telescopes, and writing about the marvels of this wondrous spinning orb from a floating observatory high above earth. Stylishly appointed, *naturellement*, in clothes from Kate Bird's fashion house, 'Couture de la Nature.' "Clothing inspired by nature!"

[*Pause.*]

Do I shock you, Mr. Wells?

BOMBER'S MOON
Deborah Yarchun

Dramatic
KATRIN, 27

KATRIN, *an American socialite, is speaking to* LLOYD, *29, a displaced, working-class East Ender. It's 1940, six nights into the London Blitz, and they're sheltering together in the basement of a music shop in the City of London. They met for the first time the previous night when they were caught in an air raid and* LLOYD *followed* KATRIN *into the basement of the music shop. They've both returned.* KATRIN *is attracted to Lloyd, but is married and clinging to her fidelity.*

KATRIN   He's cheating on me. Last night, before we met, I spied on him They have these beds in the basement of the Savoy. Extra safe at night. He was extra safe with another woman. Thing is. She's not the only one, is she? She hasn't been the only one. That's the kicker. And everybody knows. Everybody knows but me. You think I'd dare step foot again in the Savoy? The worse the joke, the better, right? You know what's funny? I spent my youth, priding myself on how I managed love. Devoted to it. Fully. I thought I understood it. I can't stop thinking of Scarlett O'Hara. I'll probably die thinking of Vivien Leigh. And Spitfire girls. And film stars. Scarlett, she's so sociopathic blasé. She comes first before anything. And there's a moment—so many moments all these women seem so free. But just a moment. Because no matter how much power they have, they either end up in the arms of a man—or a firing squad or a farm, but missing a man. It's funny. Funny. Almost. Or mostly sad. They have the power to inflame the hearts and freeze the minds of men. But they always end up needing them.

BOTTICELLI VENUS
Don Nigro

Dramatic
SIMONETTA, 20 or 40

NATALYA *is Russian and works at an art museum, but her son's death has caused a mental breakdown in which she locks herself in her apartment and imagines she is* SIMONETTA VESPUCCI, *the young Renaissance woman who was the subject of many of* BOTTICELLI's *paintings. Here she is imagining that she is* SIMONETTA *speaking to* BOTTICELLI *about the Russian woman she seems to remember she will be in a future that is actually* NATALYA's *past. For purposes of this monologue, you can imagine that you are* SIMONETTA, *age 20, in Renaissance Florence, trying to explain to* BOTTICELLI *a strange hallucination she keeps having that she used to be somebody else in the future, or* NATALYA, *age 40, imagining she is* SIMONETTA.

SIMONETTA   I used to be somebody else. Of course, everybody used to be somebody else, but although I was once somebody who wasn't who I am, except that hasn't actually happened yet. Once upon a time there was a girl named Natalya who lived in Siberia which she loved very much but her dream was to come to America and be a great artist. And when she was nineteen years old, she got a scholarship to study art at a fine American university. And she loved America almost as much as she loved the paintings of Alessandro Botticelli. And one night she was walking home through an orange grove at three in the morning, thinking about the orange groves in Botticelli's paintings, when there was a sudden flapping of wings, and the giant dark thing came and covered her. I still have nightmares about it. The creature throws me down in the dirt. He has the hindquarters of an animal. There might be two of them. Someone is clutching my hair. Another hand around my throat. It happened to the Russian girl I used to be in the future. She decides to go home and try to forget what happened. She'll concentrate on becoming a great artist like Botticelli, and nothing else will matter. Then this girl Natalya discovers that she's going to have a child. So she found a job at an art museum so she could buy food and diapers for her baby, and she almost never had time to paint again. But she was intelligent and beautiful and people liked her and she knew everything about art and she was very good at her job although perhaps not quite so good at being a mother, even though I loved my little boy desperately, hopelessly. Not yet. In the future. When I'm this poor Russian girl. This is the Renaissance, and I am the Botticelli Venus. Cupid is my son by Mars. He's really a very bad little boy. Always restless and unhappy, like his mother. She tries from the beginning to encourage him to be an artist, like she wanted to be, but he prefers running in alleys and climbing other people's trees and peeking in windows and breaking into houses at night. She was very busy at the museum and she told herself he would grow out of this, but it only got worse. When he was a child he was forever asking her who his father was, and she would tell him it was a wonderful artist named Botticelli, but when he was old enough to realize that was a lie, he never trusted her again. And she got an important job in a museum in New York, but her son hated it there, hated everything about his life there, and then one day, when he was nineteen, the same age she was when he was born, they had a very ugly quarrel about who his father was, and she'd had too much to drink, and she got angry and finally told him what happened in that orange grove. And her son just walked out the door and disappeared. He didn't say goodbye. He didn't tell her where he was going. He just left. So she was alone. And every night she would come back from her job at the museum and close the door of her apartment and pour herself a drink, and study the paintings of Botticelli, and gradually she became, in her head, the person she really was, all along. For who she really was, was Simonetta Vespucci, the girl in the paintings, the beloved of the painter Botticelli. You painted me over and over again. I was the Botticelli Venus. And you loved me very much. And now she lives forever in the Florence of Lorenzo de' Medici, in the paintings of Alessandro Botticelli. And all that other life is just a dream.

A BRIEF HISTORY OF PENGUINS AND PROMISCUITY
James McLindon

Comic
JULIA, 20s–30s

JULIA *is a Harvard professor of linguistics, currently immersing herself in Tahitian. She is usually demure, but when the situation demands, her tart tongue and athletic physique stand at the ready. Oddly enough for present-day Vermont, she speaks with an upper-class English accent. Today, her husband ALBERT is introducing her to KING, the man with whom she had an affair seven years ago in Paris while under the influence of the most powerful aphrodisiac known to man, an affair she deeply regrets. ALBERT knows nothing of the affair. Nervous, and also under the lingering effects of the aphrodisiac, which loosens all inhibitions, she tries not to say too much—and largely fails. JULIA initially addresses ALBERT, then KING, then back and forth between the two as indicated.*

JULIA You've told me so much about King, darling, that it feels like we've already been intimate.

[*Horrified realization of the double entendre.*]

Friends, I mean, not "intimate" intimate, I just feel like I know him. But not in a biblical sense, of course, how could I? [*To KING.*] I've never laid you before. Eyes on you.

[*Appalled pause, then to ALBERT.*]

The reason for that slip of the tongue is Tahitian rather than Freudian. It's fascinating how their propositions—prepositions!—how their *prepositions* always follow their nouns: never laid you before, eyes on. Fascinating. [*Pause then to KING.*] It's hard to believe: you're Albert's best friend since Harvard and yet we've never mated before.

[*Another appalled pause, then to ALBERT.*]

Met before. In Tahitian, you see, the word for met and mate is actually the same. Which may go a long way toward explaining their legendary promiscuity. [*To KING.*] Why *have* we never, ever . . .

[*Struggling to get it right.*]

   . . . metted before, Mr. King?

BUMP

Chiara Atik

Dramatic
CLAUDIA, 30

CLAUDIA *tells her parents why she is not going to have her baby in a hospital.*

CLAUDIA   I'm gonna tell you a story. And I'm not saying it to scare you, ok? So my friend Mel is 40 weeks, she loses her mucus plug. So she goes to the hospital, they admit her. She has very light contractions, for a long time, and so they start her on Pitocin to speed up labor. They give her an epidural, she watches a movie, everything is fine. Until she starts getting shaky. She's just shaking. Not really sure why. And then a monitor starts going off and the nurse tells her the baby doesn't like the side she's lying on, so they make her lie on her other side. But the baby doesn't like that side either. So then they make her get on her hands and knees and hold the bed. Like on all fours. And she's *shaking.* So then *four more* nurses come in and they decide they need to get the baby out. They wheel her into the delivery room, still on all fours, her gown just *open.* For everyone to see. Not that she cared at that point, she's just shaking in terror. So then they break her water, with a *metal hook.* And they tell her she *has* to push. So she's pushing and pushing and pushing. And not making progress. And her husband got really freaked out because literally her *eyes were rolling in the back of her head.* He was begging them to do a C-Section and they were just like "No, she has to push, she has to push." For *hours.* Like she literally begged her husband to slit her throat. The baby was crowning but they couldn't get her head out. The baby was just stuck. In the birth canal. At this point it was Tuesday night. She'd been in labor since *Sunday.* And the baby got so stressed she started to produce meconium. It's what babies poop before they've ever had food or milk. So the baby produces meconium but because she's *in* the birth canal it all went into her mouth. So when they finally DO get her out—via vaginal *incision*—the baby wasn't even crying. She was just. Silent. Because her mouth was full of meconium. NONE of it would have happened if they hadn't forced the Pitocin. *That* is why I'm not going to have a baby in a hospital. I wanna do it at my own pace, in my own house like women have been doing for thousands of years.

CATCH THE BUTCHER
Adam Seidel

Dramatic
NANCY, early to mid-40s

NANCY *finds herself face to face with the man who could be the love of her life. Thing is, she's tied up in his basement and he's got a knife to her throat, ready to turn her into his twelfth victim.*

NANCY   Look, I know why you've been doing what you do, Bill, and it sure isn't to rid the world of ugliness. You do it because you're punishing yourself. I understand it because I do the same thing. Except I punish myself directly. Two years ago I was driving down the road and I heard this voice in my head. It asked "Are you happy with who you are?" I'd always assumed I was. But that voice got me thinking. And I started looking at my life, who I was, where I was headed, and the more I thought about it the more I got scared. Because once I started peeling the layers back and I really looked at my life, I realized I had nothing, Bill. I was nothing. My existence consisted of buying things eating food being average. I was just another person sleep walking to their grave. So I decided to steer into a wall. And that's when it started. My search for feeling something. Feeling anything. Even death if it came to that. It became an addiction that's consumed me ever since. And I've tried everything. Eating pills, drinking drain cleaner, walking into oncoming traffic. [*Beat.*] I kept surviving and I couldn't understand why. But then I read your poems. And I knew the answer was with the man who wrote those beautiful words. Because he knew my emptiness. So I did everything I could to find you. Sat in every park, waited at every bus stop, walked down every abandoned trail. And then you came to me, Bill. Ever since you did, that missing feeling is gone.

CHELSEA PERKINS
Aren Haun

Seriocomic
EMMA, early 30s

A bookstore. EMMA is standing at a podium, addressing an audience.

EMMA   I wrote this book during a dark time in my life . . . a few months ago. I needed an escape . . . a distraction . . . an . . . I don't know . . . It's so easy to get overwhelmed by the daily struggles . . . the struggle to exist . . . to survive . . . always worrying about money . . . about love and family, success and failure . . . about doing something important and meaningful with our lives . . . So much of the time we're in conflict . . . unable to reconcile the past, daunted by the future, unable to cope with the present. It gets so tiring to just . . . to put something positive into the world. We've gotten so overwhelmed, in fact, that we've given up. But we still need something worth fighting for. And if there isn't anything true to fight for, we'll accept the false. The fiction. Something. Anything, to relieve the burden of the knowledge of our own helplessness. We're only human, after all.

We're animals. And as such we have basic needs and requirements . . . to be held, to be touched. We seek love and affection . . . and sex. Sex above all. We want sex. We crave sex. And that's what Chelsea Perkins is about. It's about sex. It's about hot sex and good sex and bad sex and too much sex and not enough sex and just everything to do with sex. And it's about women. Who live in a city. And it's about the dangers of veganism and how a beautiful fashion model turned exposé writer overcomes a life-threatening eating disorder and inadvertently solves a brutal homicide that may or may not have supernatural implications. Thank you for coming. If you like, I'll be signing books for the next half-hour.

CLARTÉ

Lavinia Roberts

Comic
MELINDA, mid-40s

MELINDA *is a wry marketing copywriter. She writes descriptive blurbs at an organic New Age cosmetic company in SoHo (New York) named Clarté. MELINDA works alongside twenty-something coworker CORA, Clarté's manager of business development. CORA is planning her wedding at work and MELINDA is "helping."*

MELINDA   At wedding two, I just simplified and had a black leather Elvis in Vegas. No regrets. There are plenty of Elvises out there hankerin' to tie the knot on you two love birds. It's not too late Cora. There is "Gold Lamé Elvis," "Black Leather Elvis" or "Jumpsuit Elvis." A vast array of Elvises waiting to walk you down the aisle. What is the plural of Elvis? Elvi? I still can't believe you are marrying someone named Chase. I could never trust anyone whose name is a verb. At least you have a wedding theme. Although, I still think you should have gone with cult horror classics of the 80s. Chase could come as Ash from "Evil Dead" and you could come dressed as Carrie. You would just need an 80s prom dress. We could even dump fake blood on you after the vows. I could wear my Elvira dress. Imagine the possibilities in the realm of cake toppers if you did an 80s horror cult-themed wedding. We can research 80s cult horror movie cake-toppers. Trust me. You are gonna love 'em. [*Pause.*] Don't overwork. It's important for your self-respect. They pay me what they think I'm worth. I work what I think what they pay me is worth. We have an understanding. You get what you pay for.

COMBAT READY
Laura Hirschberg

Dramatic
DIANA, 25–34

DIANA has just signed up for another tour of duty with the army. Her husband thought he was getting his wife back after her first tour ended. He demands an explanation and DIANA does her best to describe the fog of war to a civilian.

DIANA The fog of war. Let's talk about that for a minute. That concept. Because I don't think you get it. [*Beat.*] No, don't be offended. I know that face. Don't pull that face. It's not just you who doesn't get it. I've had C.O.s who wouldn't know the fog of war if they were drowning in it. They think they know. The total uncertainty, disassociation, yes . . . fogginess of battle. But what's battle? What's battle and what's the day-to-day regular shit over there? One of my dad's go-to—I dunno what you'd call it—anecdotes? Whatever. He used to say every day he spent in the army was a snafu Situation Normal. All Fucked Up. And I'm not selling this well. I know. Look, sweetheart, I know it's hard to wrap your mind around my signing up for another tour. It's not what we discussed. It totally screws with our timeline. And I love you and I loved our timeline. Love it. The house and the baby and the mortgage and all that. That's still on the timeline. But I'm not there yet. I'm still in the fog. I guess I was in the fog when we got married. And that was before my first tour. So I guess the fog extends a bit further than the writers write about. Or the recruiters tell you. Not that I was so passionately recruited. Had to claw my way into the infantry, you might recall. Practically beg to be included. Please oh please let me get shot at on behalf of my country. I promise my lady parts won't disrupt the unit's esprit de corps. Or no, I don't promise that because maybe the unit's esprit needs a little disruption. And that's the angry young private you married. The more fool you. And now I've crawled through the mud and I've dragged my shit through the sand and I've dragged my buddy's shit through the sand when he couldn't carry it because someone had to carry him. And they say in the fog of war, that's when women in the unit aren't distracting, aren't damsels in distress waiting to happen. Everything's confused so who cares if the person next to you is smaller, could be someone's mother, pees sitting down. What counts is does she have your back, do you have hers. Who is that next to you anyway? Do you know her? [Beat.] I know I've never talked to you like this before, baby. About over there. I like to think I've been protecting you, but really I wanted to keep it as just mine. Because you see, the fog, I'm in it now. It's where I live. And I like it. It's where I live.

CONFEDERATES

Suzanne Bradbeer

Comic
STEPHANIE, 40s–50s

STEPHANIE *is a seasoned political journalist. The media outlet she works for has recently offered her a buyout. Here, she has just scored a big interview with the newly ascendant presidential candidate, Senator Trevor. It is the middle of the night and* STEPHANIE *bursts into her younger colleague* WILL's *hotel room. They are on the campaign trail.*

STEPHANIE   I knew you'd be up, I knew it, we're cut from the same cloth you and I—you're working on something, me too, but don't you need a break? C'mon, you owe me, I need ten minutes of company—I've got news, baby, I've got some major breaking news! Senator Trevor's giving me an hour tomorrow. On the plane, just the candidate, just me. Crazy, right? He came down to the bar after you left, we spoke for a few minutes—and I'm in! Apparently he read this article I did on Thomas Jefferson's favorite vegetables—it was a very esoteric piece needless to say, but it turns out that Senator Trevor is a huge Jefferson fan *and* an amateur gardener, so hey! I mean, for me, Jefferson—he's my least favorite of the founders—I prefer Adams, I prefer Franklin, I even prefer that nutty Alexander Hamilton but none of *them* got me an hour with Trevor, so fuck 'em. Can we be honest for five seconds, you and me? This business is so freakishly competitive and believe me, I like competing as much as anyone but, sometimes . . . don't you want to turn all that off? Or maybe it's just me; maybe I'm the only obsessive who can't talk to anyone without wondering what their angle is. Because if I'm being honest—as much as anything—I am just so relieved. That damn buyout, it shook me up, more than I expected, it really knocked me off my game. But in that five minutes with Trevor, I was back, I was on fire, he didn't have a chance. Am I wrong? To think Senator Trevor could be special? I want him to be special. [*Pause.*] This guy Trevor—they don't make 'em like that very often, he's once in a generation. Okay, off the record and nods to impartiality and I can-and-will check my feelings at the door tomorrow—but—I feel so lighthearted! I do! And it's not just that I got the interview, although that will be the stuff of legend! It's that every now and then and in spite of our very best efforts, America produces a real gem. Listen to me, sounding all idealistic, just like you, God, I'm happy!

DAY OF THE DOG
Daniel Damiano

Dramatic
JULIANNE, late 30s–40s, Caucasian

VADISLAV, *a somewhat enigmatic canine relations specialist, has been hired by* PAUL *and* JULIANNE *to help curb the violent behavior of their dog, Carrot. While much of the play consists of* VADISLAV's *questioning each as to their relationship with the dog and each other, new depths are explored when* PAUL *openly accuses* JULI-ANNE *of submerged hatred toward the family, with the exception of Carrot, with whom she reveals a personal identification.*

JULIANNE   GOD DAMN YOU, THERE IS NO HATRED IN MY HOME!!

[*A still moment.*]

You have the audacity . . . My God, you'll never be able to fathom what's . . . You've never known what it's like to be part of a family and feel alone, let alone feel it twice. You had everything since the womb, Paul, and yet all you've become is resentful of me, and all I did is come from nothing and make something of myself. I was adopted by cretinous parents in a disgusting home, and look at what I've accomplished, and yet all I am in this house is someone who's capable of hating her own family?! A daughter I helped to raise, a husband I used to . . . to . . . Only to be . . . only to be excluded?!

[*A beat.*]

You have not a clue, Paul.

[*A considerable pause. She becomes choked up in this rare, vulnerable moment, though she gathers somewhat, before speaking to no one in particular, at first.*]

I was on my way home one day . . . after meeting with a client. It was my highest paying job to that point and, yet . . . I felt so empty. Maybe because . . . I knew what I was coming home to. So . . . on my way home, I happened to drive past an animal shelter, which I'd been by before. On this day, though, I guess, I felt . . . like I was returning to my roots or something. Like I had to go back to save myself. I saw all these poor eager dogs. Jumping up, barking, crying out . . . My God, what they wouldn't give for someone to just . . . to . . . you know, just take them home. I'd never even had a dog, but . . .

[*Slight pause.*]

And then . . . I saw Carrot. Alone in that cage, with . . . with his poor ear. So solemn, but so beautiful. It was . . . unacceptable to me that he was there, on that yellowed newspaper . . .

[*As if transported to the moment.*]

And there was no doubt that he belonged with me. It was . . . it was as if we were soul mates. God, he saved me as much as I saved him. I needed him to . . . protect, and to have a sense of protection myself. My whole life, I've always felt that I had to protect myself. Guard myself. I had no one else. I didn't as a child . . . and I don't anymore as a wife, but . . . now I have Carrot.

[*To Paul, near tears.*]

That's not hatred.

[*A beat.*]

That's . . . that's the only love I know anymore.

DEAD AND BURIED
James McLindon

Dramatic
BID, 40s

In a New England cemetery, in autumn, BID, the cemetery super-
visor, is telling PERDUE about the child she surrendered to her
ex-husband. BID is a plain, strong, middle-aged woman dressed in
work clothes. As is her habit, BID blurts out what she has to say as
if she just wants to get it out and stop talking as quickly as possible.
BID's speech is thus generally clipped, so much so that she drops
many words. (These unspoken words and word fragments appear in
parentheses, usually at the beginning of her sentences, to clarify her
meaning, but should not be spoken.)

BID   Can you see me with a child? After I came home from the
war . . . I wasn't the kind of person (that) could hold someone
else close. No, ma'am. There're some things you see in this
life that are just forever in your head. Can't unsee 'em. After,
(you) just can't do some of the things you might've done
before. After I came home, (I) couldn't even hold a man sober. (There)'s no way I could've held a child. But I drank back
then. And, turns out, (you) get drunk every night, you find
yourself holding a lot of guys, 'n' pretty soon there you are,
three months late.

[Off Perdue's look.]

Well, don't be that surprised. I used to dress better. (That)'s
why I got married. He was ex-military, too, seemed like the
right thing to do. But I couldn't stop drinking back then,
didn't even want to. After the baby came, he took her and
moved away. (I) coulda stopped him, but I didn't. (It was)
best for all concerned. Realizing that's what got me sober.
He calls once in a while, tells me how she's doing. Pamela,

she don't want to talk to me. Never even occurred to me she might want to see me, till I met you. But I'd just mess it up. Look how I messed up with you. (It) wasn't meant to be, I guess. Sometimes you need to leave well enough alone.

DEAD AND BURIED
James McLindon

Dramatic
PERDUE, 18

In a New England cemetery, in autumn, PERDUE, a new cemetery worker, tells ROBBIE, another worker, about growing up in foster homes and why she's come to this New England town. PERDUE is quiet, guarded, and watchful, but with some attitude when necessary.

PERDUE   I never knew either of my parents. When I was, like, two, my mom set our apartment on fire, cooking up her heroin or crack or whatever. Everything she had in the world burned, except me. I wasn't adopted, DYS took me and stuck me in a bunch of foster cares. For, like, my childhood. I never saw my mom again. I mean, she was a heroin addict, Robbie, they don't make model parents. All I remember is, I'm being held by a woman with this really curly, strawberry-blonde hair, only she doesn't have a face. I mean, I can't remember her face. It's like it's blurred out. I'm not even sure that was my mom. All our pictures burned in the fire. Foster care is where I learned to read faces. Cuz you have to figure people out real fast. Whether they're nice. Whether they hit. Whether you shouldn't be alone with their boyfriend. [*Pause.*] The last one, she was okay, kept me for four years. But when you turn 18, you're on your own. For her, I was I was sort of like her McJob. She got $17.00 a day for me. A week before I turned 18, she told me I couldn't stay cuz she needed my bedroom for a new kid. That's the only way she can get by. I mean, she gave me a few weeks cuz she felt bad she hadn't been able to bring herself to tell me sooner. I could've gone to a transition home, but fuck that, so I just left the next day and came here, looking for my Mom. She was arrested here. "Open container, violating a railroad right of way." Sucking Bud on the tracks. That's my mom.

DEAD MOVEMENT
John Patrick Bray

Dramatic
RACHEL, 30s, a pastel goth who keeps a vial of blood on her necklace

RACHEL *is the clerk and manager at a residential hotel for wayward souls. She has just met PATRICK, a new resident in his early 40s, who has asked for a second room, possibly to store a suitcase full of bones. She decides he's joking. She asks him to name three things that irritate him, claiming she asks this of everyone and has a list of her own. He tells her his greatest wish is to disappear.*

RACHEL   Ha! You really are morbid. [*Beat.*] I think we all kind of want that, right? So, I went to college in the next town over. And I kind of . . . hated the scene? That's when I got the job here. Being here, like, kept me away from there and also like kept the owner away from here, which is a good thing. Because he kind of sucks. Town hates him. They want to make this place like an historical landmark so no one can live here, but that's not because this place is that old or fascinating . . . I heard it was like a WPA project, but I dunno. It's really so they can like kick the owner out. But since I'm here, he's not, we can carry on business as usual. Make sense? [*Beat.*] So, anyway, in college, I was trying really hard to do that . . . notice me/don't notice me thing we all do. But I was also commuting from here which gave me this extra layer of invisibility. I wondered what people might think of me. You know? Was I secretive? Mysterious? I wore a lot of eye liner, too. To add mystique. But, what I realized is that no one actually really looks at each other. Or if we look at someone it's just to make sure they're looking at us in a way that we want them to look at us? And I find that much more interesting, so I watch people watching people. I watch the watching. It's more fun and it takes the pressure off. That's common sense, when you have a look that works you keep it. [*Beat.*] I think if I wanted anything, it would be to turn into a cat. And sit right there on the counter. And get head scritches from anyone coming in. Curl up near the bell. Open my eyes with severe disapproval anytime it rings. And just . . . take it all in. You know? That's my number one on my list. Not being a cat.

DELTA IN THE SKY WITH DIAMONDS OR MAYBE NOT
June Daniel White

Seriocomic
DELTA, 20s–30s

DELTA *fell off the top of the Empire State Building trying to catch a wedding bouquet and is waiting for* GOD's *decision as to where she will go—Up or Down. Here, she berates* GOD, *who is less than sympathetic to her claim that she was raped the night before the wedding, for not getting women.*

DELTA   This is so typically how men think! If you were a woman, you'd think differently! When are you going to get us, God? When are you going to get women? There's a lot of the Old Testament still in you. We are created in your own image. And if you don't change, we don't change. Anyway, I don't remember much about the actual—yes, rape. Because all that time—while he was doing that to me—I was crawling through the snow—the cold—searching—and I would find one person—and he wouldn't be breathing and then another—and she wouldn't be breathing. And then my mother . . . And I got through all 33 people and then I just—I started all over again. Searching for . . . And I realized I was looking at the rest of my life. And no matter how many times I would start over, it would never end. This is not going to end well either, is it? I see what you're doing. Leading me back through life things. Look, I know I don't attach and I never will. I don't believe in it. We don't believe in the same things, you and I. So this is never going to work out. There's nothing for me up here either. Dying didn't get me any-where.

THE DIVORCÉE SHOWER
Lavinia Roberts

Comic
ANDREA, 30s–40s

ANDREA *celebrates her upcoming divorce.*

ANDREA   Thank you so much, for coming to my Divorcée Shower. All of you. I just can't imagine going through this divorce without you! Oh, oh, I have been working on my vows. I, Andrea Collins, promise to practice self-care, self-compassion, and self-love, from this day forward, for better, for worse, for richer, for poorer, in sickness and in health, to love and to cherish myself, till I die. Oh, of course! I don't want to forget about the honeymoon, with myself. So I was thinking, for my romantic rendezvous for myself, that I would maybe take a weekend at Heavenly Spa Services. Maybe Pure Bliss massages. Although, I hear Las Vegas is great this time of year. Well, while everyone is here, I have something wonderful to share with all of you. A surprise. About the little bundle of joy, I am not expecting. That's right! I've decided not to have any children! None. Zero. It's the least I can do for the planet. I am so excited. I mean, I've always meant to not have children, so this is just a dream come true! I know I am going to be excellent, at not being a mother. It just comes so naturally to me, my lack of maternal instincts. So, as far as gifts for the "no baby shower." I am registered at Macy's, but feel free to get anything on the list. It's just the usual, type of things on a "no baby shower" registry. I am going to need a great alarm clock, for sure. For all the extra, full nights of sleep, I will be getting. Oh, and a new bikini. For all the extra vacations, I will be able to afford and have time for, not having any kids. Everyone ready for ice cream straight from the carton? Oh, and we still have the three tiered "just divorced" cake. Isn't the decapitated groom cake topper adorable? It's time I put on my tiara, boa, and "divorced diva," stash, and get ready for a night on the town! This divorce debutante is ready to for a night to remember! Here comes the ex-bride!

(DON'T) LOOK AT ME
Molly Goforth

Comic
DAWN, 40s–50s

DAWN *is a QVC customer service operator who loves her job
and venerates the company she works for. She lives in semi-rural
Pennsylvania and is devoted to her husband and her pets.* DAWN
*has a huge heart and a tendency to become emotionally involved
with customers who call to place orders, as she is easy to talk to and
invites confidences.* DAWN *is unsophisticated and sincerely awed by
the QVC on-air hosts, but she is no dummy. Plainspoken and clever,
she eventually facilitates the rescue of* DOLLY, *the play's heroine.*
DAWN *also serves as the narrator of the play, a responsibility she
takes seriously, as it is not unlike hosting a show on QVC. In this
scene* DAWN *explains her role to the audience and instructs them
regarding how to behave at a live performance, although her quick
mind and natural volubility and enthusiasm result in her revealing a
fair amount about herself as well.*

DAWN   Hi, everybody, I'm Dawn, welcome to "Don't Look at Me."
I mean, you can look at me, that's just the name of the play.
Okay. Sorry, I'm not used to talking in front of people like
this. I couldn't get my husband to come—he won't watch
anything but horror movies and those shows that everyone
loves about those special cops they've got for rapists and
child molesters. You know what shows I'm talking about?
There are like six of them. My friend Therese says at least
he's not like her husband, watching porno all the time, but
it seems to me there's a naked woman in practically every episode of these cop shows: just cut up and dead. My
husband can't get enough of them—he loves anything to
do with shooting stuff or stabbing stuff or cutting stuff up.
It's all I can do to stop him from bankrupting us every time

they got some kind of fancy knives on *In the Kitchen With Bob*, which is a show we have at QVC hosted by Bob Bowersox who is one of our really popular hosts, and also he is a musician and a songwriter and once at a Christmas party he did this Christmas medley where he sang "Mary's Boy Child" with Bob Venable who is another host at QVC and he also emcees the Miss Philadelphia pageant? And I just went ahead and cried right there at the Christmas party, they did such a pretty job. I told Bob later how pretty it was and he was so pleasant, just like he was anybody, not a host of one of our most popular programs that's been running for eleven years. Sometimes I think it would be nice to be married to a real sensitive man like that who likes music and cooking. You know, Bob Bowersox has won all kinds of awards and he was in that movie *The Sixth Sense* which was a real sweet movie about being a good mom even though it was scary and there was some gross stuff and I wouldn't show it to kids, just so you know. Anyway, so here's the beginning of this play and I'm going to be kind of guiding you through because we don't have much set or anything so you might not know when they're in a restaurant or something, which sometimes they are, and also other spots they go to. I'm excited about this because it's kind of like being a host, which of course I don't do at QVC, I'm Customer Service, which is great, don't get me wrong, and I love everybody there, except Shenelle who gets on my nerves but God gives us all our cross to bear and we should remember when we point a finger we got three pointing back at ourselves. Sorry, I'm rambling on. Anyway, I was thinking and thinking about how to start this story because to be honest, it's kind of weird, almost like one of things you'd read in the *Weekly World News* where they say that a kitten killed a man or something, which is unlikely, although I wouldn't put it past a cat, I'm a dog person, myself. But anyway, this is a weird story, but I think you'll like it because people love weird stories, at least going by the all email forwards I get from my mother-in-law every day, about people exploding while making phone calls at the gas station and stuff. So now I'm going to be quiet but later I'll be back to help if you get confused and I also show up later and talk normally as myself. You'll see. Enjoy the show and please don't talk or anything because we can hear you up here.

THE DOUCHEGIRL PLAY (BETTER NAME PENDING)
Duncan Pflaster

Seriocomic
IRMA, late 20s

IRMA *is talking to her old friend* MARIAH, *who thought she was dead (which she may or may not be).*

IRMA   I'm not dead, I just ran away from home. After I got out of high school and Dad died, it was like my mom turned into a total mega-bitch, you remember. And then I met this really hot guy named Peanut Butter. He was really cool. Well, in retrospect, he had a really cool motorcycle. And he was going on the road, who knew where, just free. A restless man. And I just thought, you know, "now or never." Peanut Butter and I eventually met up with some friends of his and we joined this group called the Rainbow Gathering. It's kind of like Burning Man? But all the time and we move around from place to place, living out of vans. Sometimes we're in the woods, sometimes we're in the desert, it's very free and everyone's so full of love. It's international, I was in Canada for a while. It was good times. Good people. We'd live off the land, whatever we could forage for ourselves, then go into town and dumpster-dive on weekends and we'd play guitar, and I'd sing— Janis Joplin, Indigo Girls— and we were all very happy and sexually free, right? But then Peanut Butter got hooked on heroin and so I eventually had to leave. It was time to come back to the real world and see what there is to see. And then I found out my mom just died and I'm in charge of her estate, whatever that's worth. Working it out now with the probate. So I'm back now, isn't that great?!

THE DOUCHEGIRL PLAY (BETTER NAME PENDING)
Duncan Pflaster

Seriocomic
IRMA, late 20s

IRMA, *who* MARIAH *thought was dead, chastises* MARIAH *for including some poems she wrote in a book of poetry* MARIAH *has published.*

IRMA   Oh RIGHT! In YOUR book of poetry. In YOUR Award-Winning Book of Poetry. My poem, the poem I wrote FOR YOU is in YOUR fucking Award-Winning Book of Poetry. Along with a shitload of my other poems! How long has your book been out? Five, six years? And nobody caught on that that poem is a fucking acrostic? You stupid bitch, I love you, but you never understood my work. The first letter of each line spells out your name. Well, your old name before you got married. "Mercurial. Arranging. Reminding. I. Abandon. Hypnotically". Spells Mariah. And so on. You're just lucky "Mariah Crawford" had 14 letters, or it wouldn't have been a sonnet. Or I guess I was lucky. Or I thought I was lucky. God, any reader who did catch on must have thought you were some kind of narcissist. How could you do this? A tribute? Nooooo, a tribute would be like what the mother of the author of *A Confederacy of Dunces* did after her son the author died. She shopped that manuscript around, as HIS work, until she got that shit published and her dead son won a posthumous Pulitzer Prize. And he's got a fucking statue in New Orleans; I saw it when I was there for Mardi Gras a few years back. So don't tell me that ripping off my work is a "tribute."

DOWNTOWN RACE RIOT
Seth Zvi Rosenfeld

Dramatic
MARY SHANNON, 39

MARY SHANNON *is a white woman living in a Greenwich Village tenement in the midseventies. She is speaking to her son's best friend, MASSIVE, who's 18, in her bedroom, warning him about bringing her son to a race riot that's set to go off later that day in Washington Square Park.*

MARY   Did I ever tell you the one about the white man and the Indian, Marcel? A white man and an Indian are locked up on a chain gang together. Turns out they're both horse thieves. These guys are chained together day-in and day-out, breaking rocks in the hot sun and over time they get to know each other's ways and habits and it turns out they're not so different. I mean these two really start to dig one another, Marcel. In fact, they get so attached to one another that when they get out they start stealing horses together, but then. General Custer comes to town. And there's all that cowboy and Indian shit goin' on. Our white guy could give a shit about Custer, he's no cowboy, he's a goddamed horse thief for chrissakes but the Indian, he's lost a lot of tribesmen and he's got family to protect and pressure from the tribe so he's gotta fight. The first thing that his tribe tells him to do is to invite his white friend up for a pow-wow. The white guy thinks he's going up there to smoke the peace pipe maybe get himself a lovely squaw but no, he goes up there and the tribe, they capture him and tie him up and make his friend scalp him. You know what scalping is, Marcel? They didn't have scalpels back then, Marcel. He used whatever dull blade was around to saw a circular cut around his friend's ears and then he ripped the flesh from the skull; they made him do this while his friend was still alive. He then chews the excess flesh off the skin, spits it out and works it til it's clean and soft and supple and fit to be used as a sort of handkerchief. He hangs the handkerchief on the bridle of the horse that he stole from the man he scalped. How do you think the Indian felt after scalping his friend? Drank himself to death out of shame within a year. What's the moral of that story Marcel? When you hate, Marcel, it can connect you to a group. A tribe as it were. You and your tribe get jazzed up together because you all hate the same thing and it feels all warm and fuzzy to be bonded by this delicious hatred but what you don't realize is that while you've connected with this tribe you've disconnected from the very fucking stardust that beats your heart and created everything you see. You think about that before you go to that riot, Marcel, and before you convince my son to go. 'Cause if he goes . . . so help me God . . .

EDUCATION

Brian Dykstra

Dramatic
BEKKA, 16

BEKKA *is a high school junior. She's talking to her boyfriend, MICK,
who is leaving their town after this school year to go away to college. She is trying to help him enter a project in an art fair at school
that he was forbidden to enter. She just offered to enter it for him,
but he didn't take her seriously. This is her pressing her point after
admitting how she feels about him, probably more fully than ever
before.*

BEKKA   I had a scare. I was late. A little. It was probably stress.
But I'm not pregnant. It's only been a month. And I thought
about it. I thought about . . . well . . . Not what I would do.
I didn't really think I was. It was more like, the thought of
being, you know, knocked up, maybe that was, or *would be*
an idea. Not a good idea but a way, you know, a way to . . .
you know. A way to make you stay. And I should want that.
I should want to . . . keep you. Here. But I'm going to be in
love with other people. Okay? Way more than I love you.
Cuz I know how young I am. But you're like, you're like . . .
Okay? You're like the best guy I'm ever going to get to hang
with. Which sucks to make this realization when you're a
junior in high school. But I'm kind of in awe of you. Don't say
nothing. But kind of. Not the least reason, because you're
sharp enough to recognize who the coolest chick there
is to hang out with and anyone else would bore you. But
that's just for now. I know that. I'm just for now. You're just
for now. I think it's better to end up with someone with low
expectations. People with high expectations are less happy.
I think. And also because I have them. Low expectations. I
mean what is there left to even do? Like our parents, and

61

their parents, they used everything up. They left us with jobs in retail. What's left to do? Clean up their mess? Try to re-cool the planet? And probably fail? Golly, thanks. And I'm afraid people with high expectations will only end up being disappointed. But look on the bright side. Look what I get to do. Maybe. Maybe help do. When I look back with my 2.2 kids and my not-as-cool husband; I get to help launch an artist. Or a anarchist. Or a activist. Or maybe just a guy who disturbs things. When things need disturbing. When there's dragons around, like now, we need dragon-slayers. Armed to the teeth. And that project of yours? It's awesome. I still think we should call it, "Art Is A Weapon" But, you're going to make people look at shit. Like artists are supposed to. And lots of people are going to hate you. Like people are supposed to hate artists. The ones who make them look at what's true. Cuz the truth sucks and you're going to make them look at it. So if I have to get in a little bit of trouble, if my dad gets all old testament , it's worth it.

EDUCATION
Brian Dykstra

Dramatic
BEKKA, 16

BEKKA *is a high school junior. She's a slam poet. This is her poem to humanity and to her boyfriend who she's afraid she has to break up with. She doesn't want to break up with him; she feels like she has to. But it goes well beyond that. We are at* BEKKA*'s core beliefs here. An awakening. A vocalization of what she thinks and not what her quite strict and religious parents have taught her. There is joy in it, and strength, even along with some trepidation.*

BEKKA   I love you, because loving you our life is possible. And not because it was written down, or given away. Not because it was prescribed by a deity, but because it was forged in our history, in our DNA, in what it is that makes us human. I love you better than any religious magic that was bestowed by a loving, caring god, creating us in his image. I love you better than that. I love you from the march of pre-history, handed down, through the ages, carried inside people like us, leading back, all the way back through branches of family trees, and evolutionary ladders, and refined like brainwaves, like speech, like blood cells, like music, like fingerprints, like spinal fluid. I love you evolved. I love you evolutionary. Without god in the way. Without voodoo. Without some safety net we think we need because, for some reason, we believe, we totally believe we can't take credit for loving each other this much because, for some reason, we keep believing there's no way we're worth it. That's what everybody tells us. We're not worth it. Not without some God handing out this otherwise unknowable gift. . . . Well fuck that. I got this gift from my ancestors. I thank them for it. And now it's mine. Just like these are my hands. And we extend our hands. We offer our Love. And it is something to be reckoned with. Not something simply to cherish, but to combine with yours, and used to move mountains! Because without it we never got here. We never existed. We never evolved.

EVANSTON SALT COSTS CLIMBING
Will Arbery

Seriocomic
MAIWORM, 50s

MAIWORM *is in charge of Evanston's road salting crew. She is talking to her daughter about a dream she had.*

MAIWORM   Oh I'm sorry Jane Jr., I was having the most horrible dream. It was about heated permeable pavers. They're a new technology. And I dreamt that they rose up from the ground and wrapped around me until I burned up. It's the strangest interesting thing. It's de-icing technology. Permeable paving is a type of, uh . . . paving that lets the water, when it rains, fall on top of it and drain right through to the ground, through to the ground below. The surface is both smooth *and* porous. Permeable paving was initially developed so that rainwater didn't have to go through the gutter and all the way under the city and all the way off-site for treatment. But *heated* permeable pavers are permeable pavers with heat things under them. So you can imagine what this means. It means that during ice storms, the ice melts right away, and the water goes right down into the ground, instead of remaining on the surface and refreezing into ice. So it just immediately solves the problem. Usually a plow guy clears the bulk of the snow, and then salt is applied. And of course SALT, of course SALT, there have been studies about salt being bad for the environment. I'm looking into it, it's a task I gave myself. So you add all this up, and you can imagine what this means. It's objectively better. They're trying them out over in Rock Island. They worked in Nebraska. I brought it up at a meeting, and there's some real curiosity. The rep from Northwestern was even interested in testing it out at the school. But gosh, Jane Jr., it would be such a big change. It'd put all the truck guys like Peter and Basil out of business. And imagine the construction. And do I trust a road like that? A ground like that? Like is this Evanston or is this Disneyton? Heated permeable pavers. I feel as though they're coming. Like they're snaking underneath us now. And they'll rise up from the ground and wrap around me until I burn up. That was my dream and anyhow. It's a nervousness. How was your day?

EVERYONE'S FINE WITH VIRGINIA WOOLF
Kate Scelsa

Comic
VAMPIRE, late 20s

The VAMPIRE *is a grad student who specializes in gender studies and literary theory in this outrageous parody of Edward Albee's classic play. Her part-time job is escorting the damned, and her latest charge is* GEORGE, *who has been poisoned by his wife,* MARTHA, *and is being transported to hell. On the trip, the* VAMPIRE *reflects on the ways in which male authors have historically failed their female characters and berates* GEORGE *for being an out-of-touch failure.*

VAMPIRE   What's interesting is that when the women get hurt it's on this small, domestic scale, right? It's never big failings. Never all the sons. Always just one son. Or one fake baby. Or the plants. I would go so far as to argue that when men write about the failures of women, they're writing about the failure of the vulnerable individual. And when men write about the failures of men, they're writing about the failure of society. So, then, we have to say that if you really want to be a good "male feminist," which, I mean, don't get me started. But if one did want that. You would need to look at your wife's actions as a big picture move. What your wife has done to you is about society. Your wife is society. And society has poisoned you. Into not respecting your wife. There's your thesis. There's your fall curriculum. It's new paradigm time, is what I'm saying. And, spoiler alert—no one signed up for your fall classes anyway. Or will Nick's. The kids are starting a new college called "Kill Your Darlings" where everyone spends their days writing manuscripts and then burning them in a fire. The tuition's low, but ventilation is a big issue. And listen, you participate in fiction, you take on the responsibility, bubs. Bubba. You're not a sixth of a character in search of fuck all. You're here willingly. And the last thing any of us want is for you to bore us right now.

FIERCELY INDEPENDENT
Kathleen K. Johnson

Dramatic
JULIE, 30s

JULIE *and* ROBERT *have been married for four years. They are not getting along. They decide to spend twenty-four hours together in a hotel room with no television, no cell phones, no internet or computers, to see if they can work things out.*

JULIE   I didn't know my humor, that's what I call it anyway, humor; silliness, whatever description you want to attach to it, I didn't know it affected you so strongly. You should have mentioned it months, years, ago. Your disgust has obviously been building for some time.

[*Reflecting.*]

Once again I feel like I'm just "not enough" for you. And you're right, I've probably acted like a dancing clown these past few years, because I wanted you to like me. I've always wanted people to like me and I was always afraid they didn't like me enough. I wanted you to like me a whole bunch. I wanted you to know that I am adorable and cute and funny and fun to be with and marvelous and what you've got from a combination of all my trying was embarrassment. I've embarrassed you. I don't know, Robert. I don't know if I can change. Being funny is my protection. It keeps out the hurt. It seems like people are determined to convince me that life is miserable and in my own way, I am determined to convince myself and the rest of the world that life is quite wonderful. When something goes wrong I make it better by laughing, by turning it funny. [*Beat.*] You know what's scary? I've married a man who is just like all those people who want to convince me that life is miserable. It's like you want to break my spirit. And I can't allow that. I guess I could rush to your knees and tell you how sorry I am that I'm funny and full of humor. I suppose I could tell you that I'll change. I guess I could beg for your forgiveness, but that's not the solution. I am what I am, and humor and silliness and laughter are all a part of me. Well, here we stand face to face with our first impasse in this twenty-four hour drama. Great start we've made. Instead of solving problems we've added one more to the stack.

FIERCELY INDEPENDENT
Kathleen K. Johnson

Dramatic
JULIE, 30s

JULIE *and* ROBERT *have been married for four years. They are not getting along. They decide to spend twenty-four hours together in a hotel room with no television, no cell phones, no internet or computers, to see if they can work things out.*

JULIE What do I represent to you, Robert? What in the world have we been doing the past four years? What do you see when you look at me? Do you wonder what I think about day after day? Does it ever cross your mind, or are you so consumed in your own petty little world that you do not have time for anything else. Take a real good look at me. Go on. Tell me what you see.

[*A long pause, and no response from him.*]

I'll tell you what I see when I look at you. I see investment. Four years of investment. I see pride. I see stubbornness, excessive at times and productive at others. I see gentleness and affection, not always expressed, but there. I see confusion and inability to comprehend just how to deal with me at times. I see strength and weakness balanced well. I see desire and frustration. I see a man whose touch still thrills me and whose arms make me feel safe. I want you in my life, but not at any price. I will not be another burden among the many you seem to have accumulated. That price is too high. I felt lucky when I got you. I thought, boy did I win the prize. And I did. And I still feel that way, but you've got to feel the same. You've got to feel lucky to have me. I know I need a lot of attention. But if my need for attention is a burden, I'm out of here. I don't want to be a burden. My life is falling apart in front of me and I'm trying like hell to keep it together and why do I get the feeling that the only person in this relationship that really counts seems to be you. I can handle my career and the changes it presents, and I can handle family and the crap they like to dump on us from time to time, but I'm not doing well with this. I feel like I'm starving to death. I'm walking on eggshells, because I don't know what to do or what not to do. If I'm funny that's wrong, if I cry I shouldn't. If you love me you love me, if you don't then let's quit. It's always been black or white for me. I don't do well with the grey matter. I need you to be my best friend. Either we're in this together or we are out of it. Either there's enough love between us to get through the rough times or we're sailing a sinking ship. God, it might be easier if it were over. Then I'd know where I stand. Where do I stand with you?

FRUITING BODIES
Sam Chanse

Seriocomic
**MUSH (short for Michelle, rhymes with "push"), 30s, mixed
Asian American/Euro American (ethnically Japanese-Finnish)**

*In a Northern California forest that seems to keep shape-shifting
around them, two sisters,* MUSH *and* VICKY *go looking for their
father, who has gotten lost on a routine mushroom-hunting expedition. After encountering a mysterious young boy who bears a
striking resemblance to their absent brother, the family searches for
the road back, tackling limited visibility and the interfamilial politics
of race and gender pushed to extremes. This speech takes place
not long after the sisters arrive in the forest, where they are quickly
separated.* MUSH *is discovered by the* BOY, *who has overheard her
referencing a certain thought experiment she has devised.* MUSH
*asks about her sister and father, and he promises to share their
whereabouts in exchange for information about—and the inspira-
tion behind—her thought experiment.*

*(Note: punctuation is intended to convey structure of speech, orga-
nization of thought, and rhythm.)*

MUSH I read about this Russian guy who defaced a Rothko
at the Tate—he just walked right up to it and wrote directly on it with a marker: "A potential piece of Yellowism." He
claimed he was part of this thing called *Yellowism,* which he
described as an art movement that also wasn't a movement.
He wrote this idiot manifesto basically saying that Yellowism
isn't art, and it's not *anti-*art, and it's not *not* art. The idea, according to him, is that when a Yellowist writes on something,
whatever he's written on loses everything it was before—it's
freed of its former meaning. A Rothko isn't a Rothko anymore, it's just Yellow—flattened. It stops being a work of art,
and becomes a piece of *Yellowism.* The yellow doesn't mean

anything by the way, he just needed a name. So people wanted to know—*why* would you do this? And after spewing out a lot of incoherent garbage the guy finally says—and this is the important part—"It is very difficult in the contemporary art world to say anything, to make people listen. It is very difficult to do anything in this world anymore that anyone will notice." That's where you finally hear what's really going on, what it's *really* about, right? It's like a howl for recognition—the cry of anguish of today's post-post-social media'd, networked world. It's so hard to *be* anything, but at the same time there's so much pressure *to be some*thing. So it was dumb what he did, of *course*. But the *heart* of it? The pain *driving* it? If you remove the idiot parts of it, there's actually the seed of a worthwhile thought experiment in there. Yellowist guy wanted to take someone else's masterpiece and possess it for himself, which was dumb and all about ego. But *this* experiment is just about that *other* part—freeing something from the meaning that's been attached to it, removing all the layers of preconceived ideas about Worth that we bring to something, and seeing it fresh.

[*Holding up the marker.*]

Wiping it. It's like . . . giving something a clean slate. No more perceived accumulated worth. Like with the Rothko—you imagine it's not famous anymore, so all the power it has just from being what people already *think* it is, is gone.

FUCK MARRY KILL
James Presson

Dramatic
ASHLEY, 18

ASHLEY *is the prom queen and golden girl of a wealthy Connecticut high school. Fighting off a nervous breakdown and motivated by a salacious rumor,* ASHLEY *confesses her illicit love for her brother. She is speaking to her brother* JOSEPH, *age 17 and a virgin.*

ASHLEY   We're not lucky at all, Joey. It's only *bad* luck that you and I . . . But, like, we all have like the same DNA anyway, right? Like all people? I love you so fucking goddamned much that I can't even breathe about it. It makes me want to fucking kill myself. Listen up: I know what comes next. And we *both* know that this is just stalling. We're going to have sex. And it's going to be beautiful. It's always beautiful when two people who love each other do. That's us. We love each other.And we'll fall asleep holding hands. You can be so kind, Joseph. And when we wake up in the morning, we'll make a plan to leave. To go somewhere else. Somewhere we don't know a single person for hundreds of miles. And we won't leave a note. We'll throw out our computers and our phones and we'll get new names. And we'll start a life together. Just us. And it'll be exquisite . . . And when things go wrong, because things always go wrong, we'll face them *together*. You and me can become adults together . . . Don't you think that'd be nice? If the two of us are together, it's going to be so indescribably perfect, we can just throw the past the fuck out. And it'll be something entirely, radically new.

FULFILLMENT CENTER
Abe Koogler

Seriocomic
MADELEINE, 31, African American

MADELEINE *has followed her boyfriend,* ALEX, *a company manager at a fulfillment center, from New York City to New Mexico, which for her is like being on another planet. She's in* ALEX's *apartment, where she has thrown out a lot of his stuff while he was away.*

MADELEINE   I get here, you're not here, it's like 2 pm, I'm alone in this fucking apartment. And it's so quiet, I mean have you noticed that, it's so goddamn quiet in New Mexico, when I got off the plane I was like fuck. I told work I was gonna be travelling all day, there's a conference call but I don't have to be on it, so I have no responsibilities, I'm off the grid, and I decide to walk into town. I started walking along the side of the road. So I'm walking along the side of the highway, or road, I don't know, there weren't many cars, it was like some fucking *Tombstone* shit out there, I think I saw a tumbleweed. There were all these weird adobe homes in the distance, and then like twenty minutes in my phone died and there didn't seem to be any town appearing so I was like I should turn back, and I turned around, and then I kept walking like I wasn't seeing the turnoff for this place, but then I thought I saw it but I ended up in this totally other, you know, land of weird adobe houses, and there was like fucking *no one* out in the yards, or not even yards, like little rock gardens. All the shades were down on all the houses and I started to get really thirsty. And *then* I was like is this a stand-your-ground state? Like am I gonna get shot by some crazy old white man if I knock on a door? And then I was like, is this when I die? Anyway I kept walking and I realized I was actually only two streets away from this place so I made it back alive in the end. Yay.

THE GAUNTLET
Reina Hardy

Dramatic
MACINTOSH, late 20s–early 30s

MACINTOSH, *a secretary with frustrated literary ambitions, is in love with her boss (a millionaire tech genius who dresses up in a robot suit and fights supervillains). Here, she encourages him to stop pining after his nemesis.*

MACINTOSH   Just sit down. Sit down, please, and listen to me. And yes, for the record, this is something I can speak about with authority. I might not have ever fought my way out of a hell dimension, but I've been in love with someone who was completely done with me. There's nothing that makes your heart more durable than mine—aside from the built-in defibrillator. There's nothing grand about structuring your life around some bitch who dumped you. It's sad when I do it, and it's sad when you do it. You can. Not. Think. About. Whoever. He. Is. I spent a third of my life thinking about someone who never thought about me. Sometimes I think I'm going to spend my entire life thinking about people who never think about me.

[*She goes quiet and introspective.*]

I wrote a book to impress my college boyfriend. Isn't that embarrassing? And you're . . . I don't know, trying to make yourself into a god. At the end of the day, I have a book, and you have a host of redundant super-powers and neither of us feel the way we did when that particular person was holding our hands. I always felt . . . like I was floating. Like nothing tied me to earth. I dedicated my book to him. That might not have been obvious. It was a sub-dedication. He would have had to remember an in-joke he made, but I don't think . . .

When it was over, and he stopped talking to me, I wanted to die. That's not true. I wanted him to kill me. The world where we were together was so bright, so enviable. I didn't get why he wanted to make us both live in the shitty sad world where we were apart. I would say his name, and I would picture him with a gun pointed at my heart and I would say obliterate me. Obliterate me. Make me nothing.

GREAT ROLES FOR OLD ACTRESSES
Andrew R. Heinze

Dramatic
ELLE, 50–60

_Five older actresses show up for a private reading of a play with the
author, but the author is absent and the script starts to change: everything the actresses say to each other ends up as lines in the play.
Spooked but intrigued by this supernatural event, the women become more and more self-revealing. Here,_ ELLE _addresses_ KIM _and
the other women. An alcoholic,_ ELLE _explodes after_ KIM _reveals an
adultery she's been carrying on with the husband of her best friend._

ELLE   Upset? Why am I so upset? I'm upset because my husband is cheating, with someone, and you know what I've
done about that? Nothing. You know what I've said about
that? Nothing. You know what I've decided about that?
Nothing. Not a thing. That's why I'm upset. [_Pause._] It's not
even the cheating, the act of cheating. That has to do with
him. And her, whoever she is. Lots of wives have husbands
cheating on them right now. Right now, as we speak, there
are husbands all across America, husbands in offices, husbands in motels, husbands in other women's apartments,
cheating. And right now, all across this great country, there
are husbands planning to cheat, or thinking about planning to cheat, or thinking about all the reasons their wives
would deserve it if they did cheat. I don't even blame some
of them. I don't even blame mine, when I look at myself.
Who I've become. I was a prize once, I was a delight. [_Pause._]
To think you're living in a snug little hut, like in a children's
book, with your one special friend—because that's how we
think of marriage, isn't it? if we have any romance in us at all,
isn't that how we think of it?—and then to find out you're
really living in a simulated hut, like an actor in a theme park?

What do we do with that? [*Pause.*] So it's not the cheating. It's the lying. The lying blows my mind. The facades. The fake emotions. The alternate reality of it. My world? My world is not any more rational on any other afternoon that it is on this one, with this.

[*Gesturing to her script.*]

Half the things people do might as well be called super-natural, they're just as mind-bending. So you're having extra sex, I can comprehend that. That does not derange my mind. Is it love? I can comprehend that too. It hurts me, it grieves me, but it does not derange me. My mind is not deranged by sex. My mind is not deranged by loss. My mind is deranged by lies.

HAPPY HARLEY
Meghan Gambling

Seriocomic
DAISY, 30

DAISY *resides in rural North Carolina at her sister* HARLEY'S *house with her brother-in-law,* MIKE, *and Mike's recently paroled cousin,* LENNY. MIKE *is opening an ice cream shop that everyone except* HARLEY *is helping with. As the three prepare to leave for the work site,* DAISY *remembers seeing a friend down at a bar and recounts to the group how the two reminisced about* HARLEY'S *wilder days, oblivious to* HARLEY'S *embarrassment.*

DAISY   Oh Harley, I forgot to tell you, I ran into Buggy down at Malone's—He was like, "what's your hot sister up to," and I was like, "I'm the hot one, Harley old and washed up, she don't party, she don't fight, she don't show her tits in public anymore!" He was talking about that time you lost your shit at Wade's tailgate on that guy that was trying to steal your weed! Remember when you punched him in the face and then poured beer on him? That shit was so crazy, everyone was like, "your sister is crazy, that bitch is off the chain!" And Buggy was like, "she is fucking lit man, she's the fucking shit!" I was like, "holy shit I forgot about that shit, yep that's my sister, she crazy!" You know Kenyatta? She got a baby by him, he always loved black girls, never heard a man talk about black girl pussy so much, it's like, "damn, what's wrong with my bush?" Wade was so pissed when you poured beer on him, he went to get his shotgun but was so drunk he couldn't find it, Dale had taken it out on the boat and I was like "what are y'all doing, don't shoot my sister! She's got regionals coming up she can't run if her legs blown off!" Mike picked you up that night didn't you Mike? Just before you could get shot.

HAPPY HARLEY
Meghan Gambling

Seriocomic
HARLEY, 36

HARLEY's husband MIKE is opening an ice cream shop in a town in rural North Carolina, with the help of his recently paroled cousin, LENNY, and HARLEY's sister, DAISY. Despite their mutual decision not to have HARLEY involved, HARLEY has been watching the three bond over the build and feels left out. Over dinner with MIKE, she defends her sordid employment history in a bid to be included in the shop.

HARLEY   I've had some pretty shitty jobs, wasn't like I woke up one day and thought, "hey I want to work at a rest home and look at old people drool into cups till they die," or "hey, let me seat y'all at this fancy restaurant and hide in the bathroom when I see a bunch of bitches I went to high school with. Or, I don't know, let me work as project manager at the dump , where I have to oversee a collection of degenerates that look like they staggered off the set of fucking Deliverance—you know, every day Billy Carlton would come in half dead, and I'd be like "Billy, you're on green glass today, not cans, not colored, *green.* And he'd be so hungover and withdrawn, he'd be grabbing all the wrong shit and throwing it down the wrong chute and mumbling about how he ate something weird when we all knew he was waiting for fucking Buggy to come with his junk. I'd have to get down there on the floor, and practically rip out his asshole, and he'd be like "well come on Harley don't get all butt hurt, you know I'm trying!" And the one day I had to leave early, the *one* day I can't be at the fucking place till close, Billy passes out on the line and I get blamed for it. Dougie fucking calls me at home and says "woman problems" ain't an excuse. I told him to take his smelly ass pecker—that ball sweat stunk up the whole god-damn office—and lay it over the conveyor belt so we could all watch it get crushed up into a million goddamn pieces and to take those itty bitty ding dong chunks and fucking choke on them and then take the choked pieces and shove them up his dick-hole till they come out his neck. He said I was definitely fired after that, but I didn't even care, I was just happy that having a miscarriage didn't affect my ability to be a complete cunt when duty called. I could be crying and bleeding and cursing God but ain't nothing gon' stop me from telling Dougie Marks to cut. his. dick. off. So, yeah, babe. Sorry I've "lost interest" in the past. I hope you can see how this venture is slightly more enticing.

HARDBALL
Victoria Stewart

Seriocomic
VIRGINIA, late 20s–early 30s

VIRGINIA EAMES, *late 20s, speaking to a Fox News audience. She's made the decision that the way to fame and notoriety is to give a "Conservative Woman's Point of View" and she thinks she's hilarious.*

VIRGINIA   What is it with feminists these days? In the Abu Ghraib trials, everyone is looking to blame the Bush administration for how such abominations could have occurred. And yet, liberals are uninterested in one vital fact: seven people were court-martialed in Abu Ghraib. Three of them were women. Now, ladies, I know we're not so good with our mathematical skills but let me throw some statistics at you. Women only make up fifteen percent of the military force and yet, we make up forty-five percent of the Abu Ghraib criminals. Why do you think that is? Feminists would like to say that discrimination leads women to "act out" in this way without mentioning that to allow women, the military has had to *lower* its standards. Even on American soil, in a study of public safety officers, those of the female persuasion were found to have up to fifty-six percent less upper body strength. These Police-woman Barbies were also found to have thirty to forty percent less lower body strength than male officers. They were also a hundred percent more likely to feel "not fresh" during that time of the month. When are we going to stop catering to feminists and their need for watered down standards? I mean, they fight for women to serve in the military and we have to save Jessica Lynch because her heel broke and Private Lynndie is sending us "thumbs up—wish you were here" postcards from Iraq. Women have to admit there are some things we're just not good at— police work, the military and parallel parking.

HERCULES DIDN'T WADE IN THE WATER
Michael A. Jones

Dramatic
CHAR (Charmaine), early to mid-30s

CHAR *is at her apartment, speaking to her cousin MAXINE, pontificating on how people don't really know her.*

CHAR   I was working long shifts at the store the getting home
to relieve Eugene of watching the baby. I was so tired, I didn't
bother to remove my make up or my contact lenses. I went
straight into the bedroom, walked over to the baby crib. I
bent over the crib, kissed her good night and went straight
to my bed. I lay across the bed like a big, heavy carpet. Didn't
remove my shoes or my clothes. I slept like I never slept
before. In the middle of the night, I felt my baby's teddy bear
up under me . . . so . . . I . . . I, uh . . . I went to remove it. But
it wasn't the teddy bear . . . just then, I realized that when I
went to the baby's crib, earlier . . . it was the teddy bear that I
had kissed, not my baby. I kissed the teddy bear.

[*She breaks down, crying.*]

It was the teddy bear . . . I kissed the teddy bear. I kissed the
teddy bear. Every day I ask God to forgive me. My knees are
raw from praying that Eugene and I can start again. I'm not
a bad person. I know I drink and stuff a lot, but I'm not a bad
person. I'm not bad. I'm not.

HERCULES DIDN'T WADE IN THE WATER
Michael A. Jones

Dramatic
CHAR (Charmaine), early to mid-30s

In the midst of worrying about how her better half is holding up out of state, CHAR is in her apartment speaking to her cousin MAXINE, pontificating on how people don't really know her.

CHAR   The short version is Toop was working late one night so I decided to run down to the corner bar and have a drink. Now, you know I don't even hang in bars, but I had been working so much that I just wanted to take a moment and breathe, you know. So I walk down there. Enter the bar. Get violated by the six foot eight bouncer, who insisted on damn near strip searching me. And I should have taken that as a sign. I mean, I didn't get searched that much when I visited Guantanamo Bay. No, but seriously. I should have gone with my gut. I go inside, anyway. I see some people I knew from the hospital—I say hello and then I go and sit toward the back. Alone. Not five minutes after I sit, I feel somebody staring me down. I look up. It's Tupelo's ex. Mean muggin like a pit bull. I didn't flinch. I just ordered a tall, cold, frozen strawberry daiquiri and proceeded to enjoy it. So, I'm sipping away and the effects of the alcohol start to kick in. I'm in my own little world, enjoying the music from the jukebox. All of a sudden, I feel this cold liquid running down my back. I jump off of my stool so fast! I look up and this heifer is grinning like the Cheshire Cat. Max, before I knew it, my hands were around her throat. And I am squeezing and squeezing. I'm looking at her face and I can see her fighting to stay conscious, but I am squeezing like my life depended on it. I see her eyes starting to dim and the only thing that kept me from chokin' her all the way out, was that big ass bouncer. She snatch me up like a rag doll. All I saw was red. I'm swinging at everybody and everything. We knocking over stools and tables . . . drinks are flying across the room. People are screaming and running out the door. Next thing I know I'm in the back of a squad car, handcuffed and headed downtown.

HICKORYDICKORY
Marisa Wegrzyn

Dramatic
KATE THE ELDER, 35

KATE THE ELDER *tells her 17-year-old self what's going to happen to her in her life.*

KATE THE ELDER   You won't go to Harvard. You'll go to Northwestern. You'll get a BA in Anthropology and Women's Studies, and when you realize that is not practical, you will cripple yourself with a Masters in English Literature. You won't leave because what you thought was pity is actually love, though it's easy to confuse the two. As a side note, you will have one pre-marital, ohh, let's call it a fling, tequila induced, with a math department grad student named Steve, and you'll regret it—mostly. Then, one morning, you'll wake up married, and Jimmy will be sleeping there, next to you, snoring, that gurgly-snoring that makes you think he's in danger of drowning in spit, and you'll love him while simultaneously wanting to elbow him in the head, gently, because it's Saturday morning and you want to sleep in too, and, no matter how many times you tell Dale to put her dirty dishes directly in the dishwasher because, guess what, it washes dishes, you'll hear her cereal bowl and spoon clatter in the kitchen sink, and those will be familiar morning sounds that, if you were to have any life other than your own, you know you would miss. You will get pregnant, ending in a late miscarriage, leaving you sad with a vague sense that you were supposed to meet somebody and missed a long-standing appointment. And, all the wonderful things you do have, you'll take for granted until the day you're sitting here, wondering how it went so fast, and how so easily it could all disappear.

HORNY BASTARDS
Sam Graber

Comic
/ATOR, any age, female, African American

*/ATOR is the subconscious of a journalist attempting to correlate the
sexual harassment of women in America to the poaching of rhinos
in Africa.*

AGIT/ATOR   hey wassup my sistahz this is DAYUMN!, thanks
again for checkin me out, don't forget to drop a like and hit
that subscribe, 'specially with all the dope swell i'm about to
rep in this here latest YouTube video. now: i know many of
youz been rockin the comments below and been like: hey,
ur app recommendations are cool and all but they getting
kind of stale and i need somethin different, somethin above
and beyond, somethin that's gonna make my Black Mamba
sistahz out here in the field go: DAYUMN! y'all need that
sizzle and i feel ya cuz y'all the only anti-poach sistahz out
here in south africa and you wanna be reppin ur cell to your
girls like: i got this on my mobile and u don't. so i got for u . . .
a brand new app that lets u beat the global stock market.

now i know what y'all thinkin, y'all thinkin *DAYUMN girl!*, ain't
no way a bunch'a bushveld beauties like us gonna rep some
global stock market! okay, but this app is like blowing away
the templeton and the vanguard, not that i know what that
means but it says it gives ur own 'E.T.F.', (?), and lets u trade
any stock with 'RHINO' in the name. half a million percent
returns! now i don't know if this thing's pickin stocks with the
full 'RHINO' in the name or 'RH' or 'NO' and i'm not really sure
what a stock is but it's getting *yield, y'all!* it's so easy even a
rhinoceros can do it! so say ur flippin through all them borin
apps while waitin to stop some hunter tryin to kill some
animal. i mean . . . dayumn . . . when u stop to think about it

that is *peasant war*, my *sistahz!* that is the man laughing at u!
u r just another bullet in his gun and that's the *real* poach. u
might bag ur own horn, yeah, u bag the horn before he can,
then u sell that horn for half a mil, then u bag half a mil percent returns on that half a mil from this here app and double
poach the poach!

and these days . . . that's kinda what the world's come to, ya
know? i got promo codes in the links below, i got serious
sponsor ups in the play store, and y'all be lovin me while
runnin ur own 'RHINO E.T.F.' and subscribin the life u always
deserved to be livin!

DAYUMN!

peace.

HUMAN RITES
Seth Rozin

Dramatic
LYDIA, mid–late 20s, a member of the Kono people of Sierra Leone

LYDIA *is speaking to the dean at her university, an impressive African American woman who is vigorously opposed to the practice of female circumcision.* LYDIA *was invited to the dean's office on the assumption that she would bolster the dean's argument with a male professor on the subject, only to discover that* LYDIA *herself is a proud circumcised woman.*

LYDIA   You want to know about my father? One night, a few weeks before the ceremony, when I was feeling unsure, I asked him how he would feel if I was not initiated. He told me that when he was thirteen and physically mature, all he wanted was to be a man. His older cousins were going to be initiated, but the elders thought my father was too young. He threw a fit and demanded they let him be initiated, too, and so they did. I asked my father: "Wasn't it painful?" He laughed. "Painful? It was the most painful thing I have ever experienced in my life. It took a month to fully recover." "But during that time," he said, "the elders taught us so many things—about the history of our people, about what it means to be a man, about how to treat women, how to have sex, how to drink beer, how to own property, how to face up to painful things in life and be fearless. And in that month we bonded with each other, the other boys and I. I feel closer to those men who were initiated with me than anyone else in the world." He told me he never understood why boys are circumcised as babies in the West. "Why would you do that to an infant?" he said. "The pain will be meaningless to him. He will be too young to learn anything or appreciate the significance of his initiation. There will be no one sharing his experience; no one with whom he can form life-long bonds." Did you know that among my people, the Kono, our original creator is female? And that men are derived, or, as we say, detached, from her. Your culture has been formed around the values of Christianity, no? Your male god of Abraham created man first, from whom Eve was derived. In the Torah and the Bible, women are second class citizens; sometimes only property. And there is great emphasis on control over female sexuality: virginity, chastity, fidelity. In my country, women may not always freely choose their husbands, it is true, but they are also not required or even expected to be faithful to them. Wives are free to take young male lovers to satisfy them, sexually, and they remind their husbands that no man *owns* their vaginas. I'm not sure it is possible for you to understand how we think. Both men and women in Sierra Leone are treated equally. Does this surprise you? We are both circumcised, and for the same reasons. To fully embrace womanhood, it is necessary to eliminate the vestige of the protruding male organ. But it is equally necessary for every boy to eliminate the vestige of the covered female organ to become a man.

IDIO

Abbey Fenbert

Dramatic
PIGEON, female, 18–40, a competitor, long-suffering, dreamy

A mysterious competition is taking place in a bus station repurposed as a military fortress, in a world where the air is increasingly unbreathable. While the other competitors fight and chaos surrounds her, PIGEON *holds forth, teaching the* FOOL *and whoever else will listen (no one) what she has learned about war, peace, and breath.*

PIGEON   None of you understand what war really is. Weapons, tactics—all to distract from the bad air. When you breathe in war-poison it sends a heart toxin through you and you have to practice strong breathing to exhale it or you have to starve it out, and you have to channel in the antidote or else the universe will turn against you. Tell across the street *that.* They have war lungs. Everyone does. Even if you live in Central. Even the silver-lungs. Even then, you have to practice breathing with intention. For peace.

[*She demonstrates breathing.*]

I had a good friend who was a dog and it used to bite my thighs when it heard loud noises but I taught it to breathe and then it almost never bit me after that. My zone has surface curfew. Twenty minutes a day above ground. They say the air is bad but they don't want to admit that we are the poison and if we learned to breathe out the particles we could stop it and we could all go outside as much as we wanted.

[*Demonstrating for the Fool.*]

Listen. See? You can hear that it's peaceful in there. It's the sound of spirit music.

[Hums.]

But when I listen here . . . Mm. You can hear the sick-noise. It's because you're in this place with all these negative energy elements and you haven't learned about strong breathing. Fools can do it too. Everything bad in the universe from war to starving to disease to death begins with a particle, small particles carrying good and evil, and what you breathe in you breathe back out and this is why all the air hurts. Breathe.

[Beat.]

No, not like that. No, no, no. Do it right. It's a bad song in here, Fool. It sounds like Hawk and Dip. It's all the bad nutrition you're eating.

IDIO

Abbey Fenbert

Dramatic
THE FOOL, female, 18–40, at the competitors' mercy, a former scholar

A mysterious competition is taking place in a bus station repurposed as a military fortress, in a world where the air is increasingly unbreathable. The FOOL is ready to confess.

FOOL   I was born in Central, a silver-lung. People don't remember, but the air used to be free. And then it got worse, and worse. And when it came too close to them and they couldn't run from it the rich found ways around it. Medicines and modifications. So here we are, the new aristocracy, the silverlungs. Scions of families who held property in Central, the most breathable of the Established Hospitable Zones. Inherited genetic class privilege. We're the only ones who can afford choke pills, and we don't need them! Why is that? I became a climber, a student. Learned what we did to the air and each other. Looked for the *why*. Why, why, why . . . .

[*Stops herself; a deep breath.*]

Maybe if I knew why, if I could understand why people chose cruelty and ignorance. Because it was a choice. From a rich garden of options that included self-preservation and kindness and joy. Could I . . . oh I don't know. Save the world? Guess I knew better. Why? I climbed. And the higher I got the clearer I could see . . . There's no *why*. What matters is: who. The *who*. The boy washed up on the shore, the woman hanged in her cell, the shriveled child who did not work hard enough for food. The girl from the underground zone, with surface curfew, who had a friend who was a dog, who breathed, who was promised a prize, who was traded for a war for a game for a process for me, for nothing, who was torn apart and died in pain, who breathed.

[*A silent moment of breathless grief and wordless despair.*]

I know this is a terrible waste. But ask yourself: What is the point of knowing any of this?

Ask: What is it, then, to which having your tooth rent from your skull is the more pleasant alternative? Ask: If nothing meant nothing, what could you bear to know? Ask: Why am I so weak?

JUMP
Elayne Heilveil

Seriocomic
RITA, 40s

RITA *meets* HARRY, *a man she looked up to in high school who became, she thinks, an actor who's "made it" in Hollywood. She spots him, with his arms outstretched, on a bridge, at the very moment she's contemplating the meaning of her life, with all its disappointments. She confronts him with the synchronicity of the moment, as she recalls all the people in her past who have been successful—then reveals her true feelings.*

RITA   I mean it's just so wonderful how many rich and famous and smart and . . . and happy . . . happy people, who travel and have children and houses and plants that live . . . and . . . and . . .

[*Starts crying.*]

I'm sorry . . . all around me people are living . . . people are loving, and who am I? What have I done? Where do I fit? And when I think like that a cloud comes over me. I tried to become an alcoholic—so I could belong, you know, to something. I even went to a twelve step program. But I had to tell the truth. I couldn't stand the taste. And I'd forget, you know, to drink. But I wanted someone. A sponsor, of my own, to call at 2 AM and say . . . "I'm lonely. Are you out there?" But I didn't even fit in with a bunch of anonymous people. Oh Harry . . . there comes a time, when you're presented with a choice—to take the leap—to jump, or not to jump. And that is the question . . . So I looked up at the sky and asked for guidance. Like divine intervention. Something to stop me, when the whole world seems to be coming down, collapsing all over. [*Beat.*] Do you believe, Harry? Sometimes, there are more things than science, Harry. Like you, and me, meeting like this, and how one moment, can change a whole life, one moment, one way or another. And you ask the questions, "Is it worth it? Can I find hope? Is there any good left?" And that's when I saw . . . a bird, Harry. I saw a bird. And you know what it did? It spread its wings and let out . . . a dump. A gooey, yellow, splat. Right on my cheek. And I thought, that's it. That's all I needed to know.

[*Looks up at the sky.*]

Thank you very, very much!

[*To Harry.*]

And I looked around, to see if anyone would notice . . . and suddenly I hear the sounds of the birds, black birds, all in a cluster going CAW, CAW, CAWING, a deathlike cackle, and right as I was getting ready . . . the fog just shifts and I see . . . you, Harry Shreiner. Of all people. The very boy, the very man, I looked up to, all these years, and admired . . . With arms outstretched, like he was taking the whole world in. And I wanted that Harry! Just as I was ready. To take the leap. Yes, Harry. That must mean something! [*Beat.*] And well, I thought I had to tell you. Is all. Just in case. In case . . . it meant something . . . to you too. If . . . "I" meant something . . . to you too. [*Beat.*] A second chance, Harry? I mean, how many chances are there?

KIM KARDASHIAN PRESENTS MAXIM GORKY'S THE LOWER DEPTHS

Daniel Damiano

Comic
KAREN, could be any age

KAREN *is the cofounder of the Site Specific Theatre Company, a no-budget experimental theatre company based in Detroit. Just hours prior to the one-night-only performance of their adaptation of Maxim Gorky's play* The Lower Depths, *their company has become divided due to a potentially catastrophic storm approaching, the instability of an abandoned warehouse as their venue and, most notably, the fact that they have not one reservation. On the verge of the company's implosion,* KAREN *attempts to emphatically remind her naysayer colleagues why they gravitated to theatre in the first place.*

KAREN   I think it sounds reprehensible, Livia! I think it sounds God fucking awful! Considering our aspirations from when we started this company, it's like handing me a bowl of battery acid and saying, "Bottoms up!" Christ, what does Noel Coward give an actor but a chance to do a fucking British accent? Or an audience but a comedic diversion before post-show fucking brandy? This play that we've worked on for 5 months, excavating ourselves to find the poetry in people that have nothing but their rotting, Vodka-fueled flesh . . . is what the Theatre has always been to us. Honest, raw, cathartic, challenging. Yeah, it's not easy. Just like this day and these conditions are not easy. Yeah, so fucking what?! Our characters struggle in the play because they have nothing but their spirit and their wits, just like we as artists are struggling—with nothing but our spirit and our wits, just like so many people of Detroit are struggling—with nothing but their spirit and their wits. And yet, if they don't have that, what else do they have? They have us to make sense of this fucking mess. They can look at this play from another time and see its relevance. And so we give life to the play that gives life to us that gives life to them. Because that's what we do. Otherwise, we're not artists. We're not what we've always said we were. And if we walk away now, we're just a buncha' fucking unemployed actors who show up to open calls of "The Odd Couple" in the hopes of playing the Goddamn Pigeon Sisters, and all the other bullshit that's dominated modern theatre the last half-century. This is what we do, and if we quit, then the dream is dead and we're just like every other pathetic boob who lives only for drowning their sorrows at the end of a work week. This is what we do, Livia! So what if it's a dangerous factory?! So what if it's freezing?! So what if there's rats that may make a cameo appearance during the performance?! So what if we get fucking rabies?! So what if there's a blizzard coming?! So what if this is our last day alive on this fucking earth! People will come to this and we will perform for those who care enough to make the effort because, if it is our last day, where else would we want to be than painting a canvas! THIS IS WHAT WE FUCKING DO!

LAY ME DOWN
Penny Jackson

Dramatic
PAULA BELLO, 32

PAULA *is struggling with her severely autistic son and confesses to a priest how she wants to run away to Paris.*

PAULA I know I don't believe in God. I don't understand why God would create someone like my son. I mean, aren't we all supposed to be made in His supreme image? What's his future, Father? What's going to happen when he's, let's say, my age? Maybe I won't be around to take care of him anymore. As for his father, well, I don't want to discuss my marital problem. God hasn't been much help, even though my mother believes He could qualify as a certified marriage counselor. [*Beat.*] No, what I want to confess to you, if you can call it a confession, is that I want, more than anything else right now, is to go to Paris. Get out of here—run away. Sometimes I'm driving in the car and I'm alone for once and I think why don't I just take the exit to Kennedy and hop on an Air France jet and just keep going until I'm right there, at the Seine river, the light still golden, even at night, because Paris is the city of light, always. And I would just keep walking and walking in Paris, past The Eifel Tower to Notre Dame and I don't care if it ever rains because it has to feel different, that Paris rain, soft and sweet and comforting. I want to leave everyone behind including my son and that makes me a terrible mother. My own husband, Dominic's father, well, he's gone. We never had a chance. And my mother is leaving for Florida which she deserves to because she has found a man who loves her but still, Florida could be France. And I'll be all alone, and I don't want to be alone even though my mother tells me that God will always be by my side. But He can't and He won't because there's no such thing as God.

[*Stands up to leave.*]

I'm sorry, Father, to be wasting your time but that's the truth. And although I just told you I don't believe in God all I know is God help me and God help my son and if I find myself one day at JFK buying a ticket to Paris. God help all of us.

LOVE AND OTHER EQUATIONS
Merridith Allen

Dramatic
SOPHIE, 30s

SOPHIE, *a study abroad coordinator who was never brave enough to follow her own dreams in love or life, attempts to make sense of the nature of love.*

SOPHIE   I was good with numbers once upon a time. Equations. Proofs, formulas—all of that. You don't know this about me. I was basically like a little calculator when I was small. My parents thought I was going to be a mathematician, or a scientist. You'd ask me anything, I could do it in my head. People saw me squint my eyes, like this . . .

[*Shows him.*]

. . . and they thought it was magic, how I'd come up with the answers. What they didn't see was, the numbers dancing around in my head. I'd imagine one of those old school black chalk boards, and I'd mentally write the numbers on the board in white chalk. I'd think hard on the question, and the numbers would appear on the board, white on black. Questions with answers. That's what I really loved; the idea that I had the ability to find a definitive answer to a problem. The thing is, as you go higher and higher up in math—calculus, geometry—things stop making definitive sense. Imaginary numbers—digits that are real but not real—dimensions folding on top of themselves so that you can't tell where something begins or ends. Proofs you could reason out for days only to find no solution in sight. That drove me crazy. Suddenly, I didn't want to do the calculations anymore. The chalk board in my head became this . . . haze of unanswered questions. Problems with no solutions. And I thought, well what the fuck is the point? That's the trouble with love too. Questions with no definitive answers. Problems with no solutions. A collage of moments that appear to have a beginning and an ending, but when you really think about it—really, try to reason it out, you find that the whole experience is a circular glob of events that mean different things to different people. In 15 years, Elliot, the planets have moved. Stars have been born and died. The entire universe has expanded. It's not that there is no love between us, it's that we're not living in the probable time or dimension in which it could actually exist in a way that makes sense.

MAKE MULCH FROM IT
Arianna Rose

Dramatic
SUSAN, 36

SUSAN *has been visited by the ghost of her ex-boyfriend. She is recounting an incident that caused their breakup.*

SUSAN   I know, I know . . . this is a lousy place for your sketches. Too much moisture. It's just—it belonged here. I needed to confine all visual reminders of you to one room. That's working great, obviously. I know I should just throw all your stuff away, but I can't . . . Because! Because it . . . ugh. I wanted to find clues. To find something good to hold on to from our time together. And no, before you ask, I haven't found it yet. Or a new boyfriend, for that matter. Not that it's any of your business. I did—love you. But what made you *you* would disappear, and all that was left was—vodka. I didn't want to marry vodka. I'd look in your eyes but you'd be—gone. I can still see you, with your thermos of "tea," driving in circles around our complex for hours and hours. I guess you didn't want to go out on the open road—didn't want to hurt anyone—except me. [*Beat.*] That night. Toward the end? We'd been so distant. The drinking was really bad, you were having blackouts. We had a huge fight that night. We got into bed and . . . that signature stench . . . liquor and cigarettes. I turned away from you. Your fingernails dug into my arms as you pulled me back. You climbed on top of me and . . . I just lay there and hoped it would be over quickly. I was afraid to fight back. Your eyes . . . gone. You rolled over afterwards and went to sleep. The bed was against the wall and I couldn't get out. Your left arm flung across me like a prison bar. I just lay there, trapped, with your stickiness on me, wondering how on earth we got to this place . . . I don't know how to forget you. You're in the plants, you know. You're in the music, the sketches, the waves . . . I guess the trick is . . . to somehow make mulch from it all. Grow something good.

MAYOR OF THE 85TH FLOOR
Alex Goldberg

Dramatic
SELMA, late 40s–50s

SELMA *runs the bodega on the 28th floor of the Empire State Building as a side gig to her main job, which is the mayor of the entire squatter community that lives in the building while the city (and nation) descends into chaos. In this scene she is trying to convince* ROME, *her former bodega employee, not only to remain a resident of the building but also to succeed her as mayor of their community.*

SELMA   You think all this was my plan? To be mayor of a vertical slum? My husband moved us here because he lost his job. Nobody in the city was hiring. But here, they promised us a chance. And they loved him here. He was a very charismatic man. He came to power naturally. Then he did what he wanted. Power can corrupt even the most virtuous men . . . and my husband was not the most virtuous man. He had his way with other women. I did not take to being wife of a . . . leader, believe me. [*Pause.*] He stopped focusing on what was important. He was distracted by his concubines, his vodka, and his flippant desires. He became violent when he was drinking, and then violent when he was hung over. He got paranoid. Tripled his security. Isolated us on a high floor so I couldn't go anywhere. Thought they were after him, and when I told him he was wrong, he'd beat me. Security didn't care about protecting me. So, one bad bottle of vodka, it could have been tainted anywhere. He spent three weeks in pain, in and out of lucidity. I held his hand when he went. And that was the last time I touched a man. And that was the day the Mayor was created. And soon the others joined me so we could protect the building around the clock. My journey twisted to places I could not anticipate, but here I am. So don't talk about your plan, or your choices. It doesn't work like that.

MAYTAG VIRGIN
Audrey Cefaly

Seriocomic
LIZZY, 30–40s

LIZZY is speaking to JACK KEY, her new neighbor and love interest, a few months after he moved into the widower Mr. McElway's house next door. She is discussing a trove of letters that JACK found in the attic, letters Mr. McElway wrote to his wife over the years.

LIZZY   Oh, I know all about that. Or meditation. Anything to keep the dark thoughts away. Richard Bandler, do you know him? He has a meditation for clearing out those negative thoughts. It's not very ladylike, but I do it, I do.

[*She sits upright, closes her eyes, inhales deeply and exhales the mantra:*]

Shutthefuckupshutthefuckupshutthefuckupshutthefuckup . . . I do a lot of cooking too. But then there's no one around to eat it, so . . . The problem is the grocery store. I'm only one person, I do not need that much asparagus. But it's not like you can divide up the package: *no, I'm cooking for one.* I cooked for Mr. McElway just about every day after Miss Minnie Faye died. We got real close there toward the end. That sweet man. I think he knew something wasn't right about me and Jesse, but he was too afraid to ask, ya know. He would say things like *you're a good woman, Lizzy . . . you go and get happy.* And then he died of a broken heart. Is there a worse way to die? [*Beat.*] Oh, my gosh, the letters. I didn't tell you about the letters.

[*She pulls out a small stack of letters.*]

I went to see the estate lawyer. He took one look at 'em and sent me home. There's no one. Just you and me. Mr. Key, I can't tell you, it's like a puzzle. I got 'em all spread out on my kitchen table, tryin' to make sense of it. Like, these . . . quite obviously from when he was in the war. And these . . . these from when she went up to Montgomery for something like a year, I think, to see about her sister back in '96, I remember Miss Alice was going through the chemo. But some of these, I can't make it out . . . And these . . . these have never been opened. Five letters. Kinda creepy isn't it? Readin' through other people's letters. It's like lookin' through somebody's underwear drawer.

MAYTAG VIRGIN
Audrey Cefaly

Dramatic
LIZZY, 30s–40s

LIZZY *is speaking to JACK KEY, her neighbor and love interest. JACK is asleep on this porch at this moment, so she is speaking mostly to herself, sipping a glass of wine and looking out at the approaching thunderstorm.*

LIZZY   I went by the school today. Looks like I'll be starting back after the summer. Ooooh, they had so many questions. Don't worry. I protected your reputation. Bob Searcy asked me out for coffee. I declined. I guess that's one good thing about being a grieving widow, you can just . . . blame it on death. He said I have nice legs . . . for a Baptist. I baked him a casserole. It seemed like the appropriate response. [*Beat.*] I don't remember the last time I was on any kind of a date. Okay, I won't lie. I do remember. Six years ago, July third, over on Tybee Island in Savannah. My brother's wedding. There was a groomsman . . . *Michael.* We danced at the wedding, snuck out, went over to the beach and watched the sun go down. Talked and talked. He told me he had big plans to open his own hardware business, and I told him he could do it too and he believed me.

And then there was the *not talking.* It was like falling . . . falling and falling over and over. Like we'd always have that moment, and I could just die right then and there, because nothing else mattered. In the morning we walked over to the coffee shop and got breakfast. And we walked out onto the pier for a while . . . fed the seagulls. He pulled me into him and I put my head on his chest and he said . . . *I will never forget you.* [*A whisper.*] I will never forget you . . . And then he kissed me and left for California. I knew we'd keep in touch,

I just knew it. But he . . . he told me his life was complicated, some girl back home. And he never made me any promises, so I told myself I had no right to feel anything. I still do that, by the way. Real *fun* game I play with myself. But you know, I wonder sometimes, if there was a way of wiping that memory away, would I do it? I don't know what's worse . . . to have a moment like that and lose it . . . or to go through life in the dark . . .

MOM, DAD AND A BAD IDEA
Sam Bobrick and Joey Bobrick

Comic
ELAINE, mid-50s

ELAINE HABER, *a married woman in her mid-50s, explains to her two grown children the reason she's reluctant to return to her marriage.*

ELAINE Truthfully, at first I wasn't really up for this venture, but your father seemed to have his heart set on exploring the possibilities of, let's call it extreme happiness. And so I went along with this, let's call it extreme lunacy. But now, after a few encounters with other people, with totally different life-styles and outlooks, I've come to realize how shortsighted it was of us to live our lives in a shell as we were doing. To hear new ideas, to be fired up by fresh thoughts, to be exposed to new conversations with some very amazing people . . . I didn't want to admit it at first, but I'm now experiencing the most wonderful and exciting time of my life. Don't get me wrong, I did get stuck with a few duds. But for the most part I've met some wonderfully fascinating people. Enthused, energetic, creative people . . . so unlike your father. There was Basil, a very gifted poet. His rhymes sent shivers down my spine. Weeping moons, heartbreaking tunes, lovers and buf-foons . . . The images he formed with just words were pure magic. Unfortunately the thirty year difference between us was a problem. He was in his twenties. Next came Spen-cer. He was an inventor, so bright, so creative. He came up with the most brilliant idea ever. Electric shoes. They do the walking for you. Sadly, during a demonstration for a Chinese shoe company, one of the heels came loose and the shoes began walking in different directions. They said Spencer's screams were heard in four different provinces. He'll be in a trauma center for at least eight years and his doctor said he'll never pee again. It seemed wise to move on. Right now, it's all about Leon, a very famous photographer. He can't stop taking pictures of me. I find the attention incredibly arousing. I have to admit, you kids knew what you were talking about. Your father and I are definitely not as right for each other as we once thought and while I don't usually like to use phrases like this, right now I'm as happy as a pig in shit. Isn't that wonderful?

MORTICIANS IN LOVE
Christi Stewart-Brown

Seriocomic
LYDIA, late 20s–early 40s

LYDIA *speaks to the audience as if they were customers at her funeral parlor.*

LYDIA   Here at Eternal Acres your loved one will be in good hands. My hands. These tiny, delicate, white hands. A woman's hands. Taking delicate, loving care of your loved one. These little hands will lay out and process your loved one with the utmost care. These little hands will gently insert the trocar—a trocar is an object that closely resembles a hypodermic needle, except it's about two feet long and three quarters of an inch in diameter—insert the trocar ever so gently under the rib cage of your loved one and suck out all of the fluids in the body cavity. Then these hands will gently replace the fluid with a lightly herbal-scented formaldehyde mixture, or "cavity fluid," thus preventing unsightly decay before the date of the funeral. These hands will then imperceptibly stitch the lips together so that there are no last minute surprises at the ceremony.

And even more important than the lips are the eyes. Carefully, gently, these hands will place under the eyelids small, rounded, flesh-colored devices that fit over the eyeball. The eyelids are then pulled down over the device and the serrated surface keeps the eyes firmly shut. It simply wouldn't do to risk the eyes opening during the wake. And lastly, the gentle, loving, somewhat larger hands of my assistant will dress the body, style the hair, and apply make-up that gives the illusion of life itself. All this for six thousand, nine hundred, ninety-nine dollars, coffin included.

MOTHS
Don Nigro

Dramatic
MEREDITH, 34

It's the summer of the year 1970, in a small town in Ohio. MEREDITH is being visited by her closest friend, BEN, age 20, whom she used to babysit when he was a child. Now, BEN is grown up and back from college for the summer, and he's come to see her. They are sitting on her screened-in back porch at night, watching moths trying to get in. MEREDITH has been in and out of mental institutions for much of her life. She's out now, living with her father and her 15-year-old daughter, whom she loves very much. She is terrified that her madness will return, and that her daughter has inherited it. Here she reveals to BEN her deepest secret.

MEREDITH   I know a secret. You've got to promise not to tell my father. It's about the moths. Each one of the moths that comes to the back porch at night when I'm sitting on the porch swing, watching the fireflies, each one of those moths is actually the soul of something. They're ghosts. Moths are ghosts. And at night they come for you. They want to get in the house so that when you're asleep they can crawl in your ears and get into your dreams. I listen to the crickets. The crickets are trying to warn me. To watch out for the moths. And the fireflies are warning me, the way they flicker on and off in the dark, the patterns they make in the dark. Because once the moths get into your head, they start nibbling away at your brain, from inside your skull. And as they nibble away more and more of your brain, they uncover buried memories, like digging up pieces of broken crockery or old bones in the back garden, out behind the shed, in that patch of ferns. The moths that get into your brain, the ghost moths that haunt the inside of your head are engaged in a sort of archaeology of memories. And these are memories you don't want dug up. Bad memories you spend years trying to bury in your head, but also good ones, that hurt even worse because they're memories of things you can't ever get back. The ghost moths get into your brain and eat away the insulation and uncover the memories and you start to go mad again.

THE NICETIES
Eleanor Burgess

Dramatic
ZOE, 20, African American

ZOE *is in her professor's office to discuss a paper she wrote. The professor disagrees with some things in it about racism down through American history.* ZOE *takes her on.*

ZOE   You're more afraid of looking like a racist than you are of *being* a racist. Don't you want to think about that? What are you doing to promote equality? Are you using the money you saved on your son's tuition to fund a scholarship for a student of color? Are you getting all your white friends together to call congressional representatives and demand criminal justice reform? Or do you actually never bother to think about racial equality, and now you're just trying to claim that you do to save face when you know you've been behaving badly, because in that case you can go fuck yourself. I want this to be your problem. I have spent my *life* living with this problem. Why are my teachers talking to me the way they do? Why are my friends looking at me the way they do? Why is this boy interested in me? Why isn't this boy interested in me? It keeps coming. Was I just imagining it, or did my sociology professor jump when I jogged past him in the street after dark? And will I ever really be safe if that's the kind of thing that happens *here? Here.* Is there anything for me to love about my country, any way for me to look around this country with love when everything is tainted, *everything,* and no one else seems bothered by it, everyone else seems happy as a clam—and I have the burden of seeing it for what it really is, *I* have to educate people, and *I* have to decide when to stop educating people . . . and just let it go in order to stay likable and employable and *I* have to try to focus on my dumb and problematic assignments with all this shit racing through my head, and it's all *my* problem, how is that fair?? So here I am. In your office. This is your problem

NINETEEN FORTY-NINE
Don Nigro

Seriocomic
BECKY, 21

BECKY, *a young wife and mother in a small east Ohio town in the year 1949, has recently given birth to her third child and is starting to feel trapped. Her first two children were fathered by a man who ran a house of mirrors in a traveling carnival. Her first husband hung himself in the barn. Her current husband is a baseball player who is often away from her. BECKY's mother died when she was born, she's never known who her father was, and although she loves her husband and her children, more and more she is feeling the need to run away and never come back. Here, she is sitting on a bench in town talking to a strange old man who runs a curiosity shop and believes in aliens. She's trying to decide whether or not to abandon her husband and children.*

BECKY My husband thinks I'm crazy. He doesn't come right out and say so but I can tell. He thinks it's weird that I wanted to name the baby because of a book I read about Benjamin Franklin and a mouse. This mouse was born in this old church in Philadelphia, and the winter was so bad, him and his parents and his twenty-five brothers and sisters were eating prayer books. So the mouse went off to seek his fortune, and he ended up living in Ben Franklin's hat, and giving him good ideas. I didn't read a whole lot when I was a kid, because the words were always jumping around on the page and the letters would get all scrambled up, but this one book, somebody used to read it to me when I was really small, so I kind of knew it by heart, and for some reason this book just meant something to me, and I wanted to name our son after this mouse, but the mouse's name was Amos, and that sounds like some old fart's name, so we called him Ben, but Johnny thinks it's weird, and he also thinks it's weird that I keep rearranging the furniture every day while he's gone, and then he gets up in the middle of the night to go to the bathroom and gets turned around in the dark and runs into the wall. But I keep thinking if I just get all this furniture in exactly the right place, then maybe I'll be happy. But somehow I never get it right.

OATMEAL AND A CIGARETTE
George Sapio

Dramatic
JANE, 20s

JANE *is arguing with* CLAIRE, *the mother of her charge,* BILLY.
CLAIRE *has just threatened to fire* JANE *for what she sees as insub-
ordination. (In the reality of the play,* CLAIRE *is* BILLY'*s older brother
who has been assuming the motherly duties since he was a preteen
and* BILLY *a three-year-old.* BILLY *is now 30 and mostly behaves like
a youngster/post-toddler but is becoming more and more affected
by his ignored biological urges.*

JANE Think, Claire. How many babysitters have you been
through? I've been here over a year, four days a week. No
one has stayed but me. I am just simply telling you the truth.
Have I ever—ever—asked *any*thing of you? Much as you
might hate to admit it, you do need me. Billy is very important to me. I care about him. A lot. And he needs me, too.
You know he needs me. He cannot survive here without a
babysitter. You want to try breaking in a new sitter? Remember how long it took before he stopped going into major
fits when you left the house? He waits at that window every
day starting at five twenty-five and never takes his eyes off
that subway entrance, waiting for you to come out at five
thirty, look up and wave at him. Because he thinks if he's
not there you won't find your way home! How will Mommy
know which apartment to go to if he doesn't see Billy at the
window? He thinks that one of these days you're going to go
to work and won't come back. He's a captive who is scared to
death to go outside, so he stays here and pretends he's still
a three-year-old. What are you gonna do in five years? Ten?
What if something happens to you? Where will he go? What
will he do?

OH NO. NOT AGAIN
Sarah M. Chichester

Comic
WOMAN, could be any age

A WOMAN is sitting at a table. She's alone. She's looking around for someone. She turns and addresses the audience.

WOMAN No. This can't happen again. He's already 15 minutes late. And I stupidly came 10 minutes early even though it's happened before so now I've been here 25 minutes and it looks even more like I've been stood up. The last time this happened I tried to play it off by downloading and playing a random app—as if I just there to eat and play a game as I ate. But the waiters knew. They looked at me like I was a sad little scraggly puppy who was lost and needed help to find her way back home. There was also the time I waited 20 minutes and when the waiter asked me for a third time if I wanted anything to drink he very politely started pushing for me to get a drink at the bar as there were other couples waiting for a table. This has happened so many times I'm not even sure which one was the most embarrassing anymore. It might've been the time I tried to make a secret run for it and I tripped head first on the linoleum floor so hard that a tooth chipped and a started bleeding. How many dates end up with a dental emergency? No wait—it's not a date as he didn't show up either. You'd think my text that I was going to the emergency room and that I had to cancel would've warranted being asked to reschedule. No, he just replied back "that sucks." "That sucks!" Seriously?! Is that really better than not getting a response at all.

[Sighs.]

The worst problem is I can't begin to just keeping ordering drinks while being stood up. I tried that, and the guy ended up showing up an hour and 15 minutes late. I had five drinks at that point. Wanna guess how great that went? And better yet he didn't even have a good excuse for not showing up late! He straight out said "I wasn't sure if I wanted to come." Really?! Couldn't he just cancel? Why keep me waiting? Is it really so hard to text that you're not coming? I have no idea why this keeps happening to me! Is it something I do? Something I say? Have all the men in the world universally decided behind my back that this was more fun to do to me than simply sit with me for dinner for what? 90 minutes?

[*She sees someone else sitting alone.*]

Although, he's also sitting alone. That hasn't happened before. At least that I know of. [*Beat.*] I've been so focused on being stood up, I never even noticed if anyone else has been stood up. Screw it, I'm making my way over there. Let's see how it goes.

[*She begins walking away.*]

ON THE HEAD OF A PIN
Frank Winters

Dramatic
ALLISON HOWE, late 20s–late 40s

ALLISON *has come to the office of the* New York Guardian's *editor in chief with a job to do. One of their reporters,* LILY STRAUSS, *has highly sensitive information she plans to publish, and* ALLISON, *on behalf of the attorney general's office, would like to know where she got it. The editor in question,* JON, *informs her that* LILY *takes her responsibility to anonymous sources seriously and is unlikely to cooperate, implying that should* ALLISON *push the matter, he'll be forced to "bring the full weight of this newspaper" down on her head. This, to say the least, does not faze her. And when* ALLISON *threatens more severe legal consequences,* JON *tells her "This isn't funny."*

ALLISON   Finally, we agree on something. If Lily Strauss doesn't name her source, my office will have no other choice but to assume that there wasn't one, and that's a whole other world of hurt. In fact. You know what? This'll be fun. You got a pen? Okay . . . You deliver, what, two and a half million a day? Plus or minus another two on your website, let's be generous, let's call it five million every day, what exactly do you imagine will happen then? She doesn't wanna talk, so you make her a hero, right? There'll be op-eds, historical perspective, a letter from the editor, and let's say for the moment that anybody pays attention in the first place, which is a decent leap, but let's say it works, then what? There'll be outrage. Protests. Drum circles will be formed in her honor. Keith Olbermann will sing her a song for a whole seven minutes, and you know what will happen when? They'll cut to commercial and talk about something else. And Lily Strauss will go to jail for a very, very long time, and eventually, nobody will care anymore, and right after that, nobody will even remember. But see, I'm hoping it won't come to that. I'm hoping you're going to be a hero, and convince our girl that she has a patriotic fucking responsibility that's more important than her ego, and if not, well, you should both know I'm perfectly serious. I could charge her with treason. The world isn't just changing, Jon, it's changed, and people like you need to start getting ready. Any questions?

OUT OF ORDER
Jennifer Maisel

Dramatic
SARA, 40s

SARA *is in charge of an expedition to Mars. Here, she is following the descent and landing of the Mars rover.*

SARA   Entry, descent and landing. EDL. First Spirit—and then three weeks later, Opportunity. From the moment a rover finishes its seven month journey through space and hits the atmosphere of Mars, there are six minutes, six minutes that comprise Entry, Descent and Landing. Six minutes of terror. It's where we say, OK, Spirit, we've sent you out to this new world because you're ready to run the gauntlet. We try to sound convinced but really, we're shitting our pants because—well you're moving at 12,000 miles an hour when you hit the atmosphere. You're supposed to send us a tone. Send us a tone. From the moment you send it it takes 10 minutes for us to get it so senditsenditsendit. Tone. Your heat shield is turning as hot as the sun. Send us another tone. Damnit—Where's the tone, where's the tone? OK. OK. Heat and deceleration pulses are slowing you down to Mach 2. Tone. Your parachute is opening. Can't hear you. Can't hear you. I can't hear you! OK . . . Tone. Now you're at 1000 miles an hour. 500. 250. Tone. Tone. Tone. Heat shield gone. Lander launched. Tone. Don't forget to fire your retro-rockets. Tone. Inflate your airbags. Are you there? Are you there? Oh my god. You're there. Slam the ground and bounce. Be careful—be careful of the rocks—they're sharp, don't—. Pleasepleasepleasepleaseplease. Slam. Slam. Slam. Slam. Slam. Slam. Slam. Slam. Slam. Roll. Rest. Waiting. Waitingwaitingwaiting. Tell us you're OK! Tone.

PARADISE STREET
Constance Congdon

Dramatic
JANE, 30s–40s

JANE, *a college professor, has been brutally beaten by a female hitchhiker she picked up. She is in the hospital, undergoing a speech evaluation. This is what she hears herself saying.*

JANE Marx. Hegemony. Thousands of years before all the writing about, One, a mode of thought, and Two, this particular word for hierarchical systems, the Mayans thought the wheel was the symbol of death so they refused to use it to travel with death rolling you along, away from everything. No wheels at all and they still invented time. And women knew it already because they tended the dead. Women were clocks themselves because of their menses and the moon was round and a wheel but someone knew it wasn't flat. A ball, some young boy played that dangerous game and said this black ball is like the moon? No. Because they died and could see themselves die in the game and not round or even a ball it's a line, a straight row of—of—Chuck Close painting a portrait with paintings Close up but far back a face of a woman who paints the Golden Mean. See? Flat. Not like a saddle. A riderless horse the bears of heaven would never ride. So how did the schism come? It's the counting, counting, counting, counting, counting, count of down. Feathers are units of consciousness, calling it time. And they kept score in the game as soon as they had time, had death. They had all the parts of time including number of breaths. And then life was a collection of units. And then life became a fearsome thing because it became only a matter of Time. Then trying to catch it, to stop it—no—and running from it and each other. And where is that watch I got for graduation? In the drawer. In that top drawer with all the pins and that cummerbund I wove in that class and spent that money to have it made into—Hopi men do the weaving so who does the fabric of the universe? Who has it? I never saw it. I'm the voice in my head that never shuts up. Only I'm someone else's voice, so NONE OF IT MAKES SENSE OR IS EVEN COM-PREHENSIBLE OR PILLOWS!

PARADISE STREET
Constance Congdon

Dramatic
TJ, 30s

TJ is at a gyno-herstorical convention. She is sitting on a dais, with a microphone in front of her. She's dressed like JANE, a college professor whom she assaulted and whose car and purse she stole. She's being interviewed by an older woman, SHEILA.

TJ   What you need. What all you rich little cunts need is a job—or two—or three because that's what it usually takes to make enough money to pay the rent and feed yourself. I'm going to tell you how to make ketchup soup, so you might want to write it down in one of those notebooks of yours. Okay—go into a Mickey Dee's and get some packets of ketchup—they just don't leave them out any more, so you need to pretend you're getting them for someone else, someone in a car. And then you say, "Oh—and an extra cup, so we can share the milkshake with my grandma." Do not say "drink" or they'll give you a tiny, crappy cup. You need a cup that will hold some milkshake and not collapse as "Grandma" drinks from it. Then you need hot water and don't go looking for it in some restroom because none of them run it any more. So leave the Mickey Dee's and go to a Cumby or a Circle-K or a 7-11. Walk in and go to the coffee maker place they all have, waving your cup, like "I just need to heat up my tea," or "dilute this crappy coffee I got at McDonald's I shoulda bought your coffee." Go to the hot water spigot—it's usually part of the Bunnamatic or whatever coffee maker they have—pour the hot water into your cup, while pocketing some salt and pepper packets and a stirrer and walk out saying "Thanks!" And then tuck yourself away somewhere outside because now you're going to cook. Empty all the packets of ketchup into the hot water, as many as you've been able to get, stir, and then add the salt and pepper because ketchup is way too sweet—and then enjoy it. It's free soup.

A PIECE OF PROPERTY
Richard Vetere

Comic
TRACY, late 20s

TRACY *is an accountant who is waiting at a bus stop and speaking to* CHARLIE. *She is very impressed that he had the foresight to buy a tiny property, ten yards by five yards, next to a bus stop.*

TRACY   What he needs right now is not a lawyer, but a good woman! A woman with business brains! A woman with the smarts and the guts to stick by him thick and thin! He needs a woman he can turn to in the middle of the night to discuss his business plans, his schemes, and his goals! He needs a woman with a mind of her own! A woman with her own business plans, schemes, and goals! He needs a woman who will look him straight in the eye and tell him that, yes! Yes, he should be the master of the universe! Yes, he should be the mogul of all moguls! Yes! He should go out there and kick butt and turn the world into his playground! That is the kind of woman he needs! And there are not enough of those kinds of women around, Charlie, so when you find one you better get on your horse and ride after her, because *she* will be your guiding light! *She* will be your stairway to the front of the line! *She* will be the strength you need and desire at your side. Forget these emotional females! Forget feelings and heartaches! Bury the sentimental, Charlie! Go for it! Take hold of her! She is yours! She is there for you!

A PIECE OF PROPERTY
Richard Vetere

Comic
JANE, late 40s

JANE is a working-class woman whose husband, CHARLIE, just bought a tiny lot, ten yards by five yards, next to a bus stop, spending the last of their savings. She is speaking to him and his best friend PETE, a mailman, as CHARLIE sits on a chair looking over his piece of property.

JANE   Pete, tell my husband I am going home. It's all over. He ruined my life. Ten years of marriage and all I have to show for it is an empty lot with a jerk in a chair smack in the middle of it! I coulda have been somebody, you know. I had a real chance to be a Rockette! I had the legs! I had the shoe size! But I met Charlie here and gave up a career in show business! Who knows where I coulda went to? I coulda been a stage actress like my great aunt Yolanda! Then from there maybe I woulda went into movies! Maybe I woulda been a big star! Maybe I woulda won an Oscar, huh? Tell my husband that because of him I ruined my life and gave up a big house in Hollywood and now all I got to show for it is a piece of *dirt*! Pete, as far as I am concerned I am a *free* woman. I say that to your face right in front of Pete! Charlie, if you still have brain left, I want you to know that your wife is leaving you. Pete, if you want to drop by for a shot of booze and a late night movie on cable, just knock. You know how to knock, don't ya? You just put your fist to the door and bang! Knock, knock, who's there? An imbecile and I married him!

[*To* PETE.]

Goodnight, Pete! I thought I married a normal man. I thought I married a guy who'd give me a couple of kids, piss in the toilet and not miss, work at a job and die of lung cancer in a couple of years. I wanted what other wives had. Don't I deserve a normal life? Don't I deserve a man with a beer gut, a prostate that works once in a while and a man who would die before me leaving *me* whatever we saved in the bank? Why can't I have that? I never get anything other people get. I was hopin' to be a widow, Charlie! I was hopin' to have some fun once I put you in the grave. You creep! Pete! All you gotta do is tap and I'll be at the door. I can't wait to get back at this, this *husband*!

PLAYING WITH FIRED
Steven Hayet

Comic
SAM, early to mid-20s

SAMANTHA "SAM" DANSBY *is speaking to* JOHN O'BRIEN, *Senior VP of J.C. Toys, the third-largest toy manufacturer in the world. After sneaking past his two receptionists,* SAM *appears in* JOHN's *office unannounced, demanding an interview for the job of her dreams: Senior Assistant Director of Product Distribution.*

SAM   Mr. O'Brien, when I say I need the job, I don't mean I "need it" need it, like I need the money or the benefits or the pension plan and all that fluff. I mean it's nice—don't get me wrong, but I can get that from anywhere since I'm smart and determined and pretty much any suit with half a brain would be lucky to have me. But I meant "I need this job" as in "I *neeeeed* it." I've always dreamed of working at J.C. Toys. It is what I've always set my sights on. Even as a little kid, I knew I wanted this job.

[*Incredibly serious.*]

Being Senior Assistant Director of Product Distribution. Sending toys to children all over the world. That's the closest you can get to being Santa Claus. [*Beat.*] So how do you want to begin this interview? Would you like me just to tell you about myself or do you have some question you like to open with, because I have two words for you: [*Beat.*] Lieutenant Liberty. [*Beat.*] Lieutenant Liberty, an action figure produced by J.C. Toys, popular in the mid to late 1990s with his slogan: "Don't Take No for An Answer." [*Beat.*] Now I may seem like a girl who played with Party Ponies or Slender Sally dolls, but I'm a fighter, like Lieutenant Liberty. When Christmas of 1998 came around, I wanted a Lieutenant Liberty. I asked my parents every day for two months. They would say no. They would say "Samantha, honey, wouldn't you be happier with a Party Pony?" I stayed strong. I would not settle for a Party Pony. I refused to take no for an answer then and I refuse to take it now.

POPCORN FALLS

James Hindman

Seriocomic
BECKY, 30s–40s

The town of Popcorn Falls has to put on a play in one week in order to receive a grant they need to stay afloat. BECKY, the only person in town who knows anything about theatre, tells MR. TRUNDLE why theatre is so important and how it changed her life.

BECKY Theatre is . . . I don't know. Okay. There was this time . . . I must have been fourteen. We were on a field trip and they stuck us all in this auditorium to watch "Romiette and Julio." A rock version of Romeo and Juliet. It had to be the worst thing I have ever seen. It was boring and annoying, and so loud we couldn't understand what anyone was saying. And to top it all off, this girl I despised, Karen Colier, was sitting behind me kicking my chair, trying to annoy me. Suddenly, in the middle of the show, the entire theatre goes black. So they make everyone go outside and wait at the back of the school on these hills. Well, they weren't exactly hills . . . I'm not sure why I feel I need to tell you every tiny detail. Anyway, after about fifteen minutes, one of the actors starts singing. Pretty soon all the actors are singing. They perform the entire show for us. No sets. No costumes. And by the end of it, I look over and Karen Colier is smiling at me. And on the bus ride back, she sits next to me and we talk the whole ride home about the play. How cute the guy was playing Julio. How sad it was at the end when they died. A girl who hadn't spoken to me since kindergarten. And I remember thinking to myself . . . wouldn't I be the luckiest person in the world if I could be a part of something that brought people together like this? To share an experience that has never happened before, and will never happen again?

THE RESTING PLACE
Ashlin Halfnight

Dramatic
ANNIE, 32

*After her older brother's suicide—which was precipitated by reve-
lations of his predatory sexual behavior—ANNIE returns home to
find that her sister and parents have abandoned plans for a funeral.
Their thinking is that their hometown will be further upset by any
public display, any ongoing reminder of the horror of her brother's
deeds. ANNIE has missed the preliminary round of decision making,
and as she gets up to speed she takes the strong position—against
her family—that they should hold a proper burial. She is speaking to
her mother, but also indirectly to her sister and her father, who are
present.*

ANNIE   You know what I do at my job, Mom? If you boil it down,
you know what I do? Against all odds, I try day-in and day-
out to convince hundreds of thousands of people, *millions* of
people, that—even though they're *hell-bent* on plastic wrap
and cheap gas and pesticides—I try to convince them that
they need to make better choices. Different choices. And
they don't want to. They *really* don't want to. They're scared
and stubborn and set in their ways. But sometimes they
have to—because their kids make them or because it's the
new law. And they get angry. And they resent the hell out
of it. Because they're really really attached—*really fucking
attached*—to small-minded, selfish thinking. And I have to
go up against that kind of thinking—and huge corporate
interests with politicians in their back pockets, usually—and
I have to listen to them yelling and screaming and calling me
a tree-hugging Swedish Canadian socialist dyke—and sometimes they threaten to kill me, literally end my life, because
of a bike lane, or water rationing, or a blocked project in the

Headlands. That's what I do, every day. So—a few people who want to scream and yell and hold up some fucking signs as we drive into the cemetery . . . well—I think I can take care of that. [*Beat.*] So. I'm sorry I wasn't here. I'm sorry I was out of touch. I'm sorry I missed the discussion, but we're having a funeral—a proper burial with a proper service—and I don't give a shit if they show up by the thousands. Let them come. I don't care.

THE ROLE
A. J. Ciccotelli

Comic
CELIA, 26, a movie director

CELIA tries to convince KEN's *partner* ROB *that he is the perfect subject for her reality TV show.*

CELIA   Well . . . it started at your audition. You see it was down to the three most interesting subjects . . . the Yugoslavian with the cane and harmonica and the lesbian bi-polar Republican and you guys. Well . . . that special something was you. He told us all about you. You're quite a character, Rob. I can call you Rob, right? We're going to spend a lot of time here. Every night for at least seven to eight months. We'll follow you around . . . in the kitchen . . . in the bathroom . . . on the futon . . . both of you on the futon. Together. You know what I'm saying? Know what I'm saying? I just need you to sign this release form so we can begin filming. I love this story . . . absolutely, love it. Ken told us about the time you and him walked through Barney's and you walked out with new evening outfits for both of you. You see that's when it exploded in my brain . . . the perfect subjects for my film . . . two normal men, living normal lives but one has a secret . . . one is inadequate in his place in the world and the other saves him by stealing for him. Yes . . . there is more. The fact that you murdered your parents when they ridiculed you about your other little secret . . . but you weren't convicted because you were a mastermind at covering up the murder from watching *Murder She Wrote*. To be quite honest it was a bit over the top but so are the Kardashians. No . . . perfect. The ugly truth. We want to put *fucking ugly* on the screen.

THE ROMEO AND JULIET OF SARAJEVO
Brian Silberman

Dramatic
RADA BRKIC, early 40s, ethnic Serb from Bosnia

Admira Ismic and Bosko Brkic were natives of the former Yugoslavia living in Sarajevo during the Bosnian War. She was a Muslim and he a Catholic Serb, but the young couple fell in love. They were killed on May 19, 1993, while attempting to escape their war-torn city. Photographs of their bodies were used by media outlets, and a Reuters dispatch was filed dubbing them the Romeo and Juliet of Sarajevo. Here, RADA BRKIC, Bosko's mother, addresses the audience in English after their death.

RADA   I raise them, all my children, without thinking about religion or nationality. I never say, "You are Serbs, they are Muslims or Croats." Never. So, for my Bosko I did not regard her as a Muslim, as different. I saw her only as the girlfriend of my son, who loved her, and who I loved, too. I lose my own husband when he is only forty-five. A heart. Is bad, his. My Dragen's heart. But we lose each other before that. Is oil and water, I say always, that we are oil and water to each other and cannot stay together even if we want. It is too much oil and water fighting to separate.

[She pauses slightly.]

And so I say to Bosko, if you love . . . if you have love there is no matter anything other and you keep it whatever time there will be. And they fought sometimes, like everybody else, but there wasn't a day they did not know, for every minute, where each other was and find some way to speak to each other. I ask her once, I was sitting her once . . . with . . . and I ask her, can this war separate you from Bosko? And she said to me, only bullets can. Only that.

SATISFACTION
Nandita Shenoy

Comic
TEDDY, late 30s–early 40s, Asian American

TEDDY *is speaking to her mentee,* CECILY, *about an unfortunate situation at their high-powered law firm.*

TEDDY   Listen, I know it's exciting and flattering and great to have someone so important pay attention to you. I do. But don't be fooled. He's using you for sex. I am the Queen of using people for sex, so listen to me. He's approaching that age where he's not sure whether he's still virile and it makes him feel good to sleep with the hot young associate. You think he's smart and powerful and that makes him feel smart and powerful. Meanwhile his wife who actually is smart and powerful goes to Soul Cycle 6 days a week to stay hot and pulls in 7 figures at Goldman. She's the mother of his children, and if she ever finds out, she will crush you like a tiny little bug. He's never gonna leave her. God! Now I sound like fucking Meg Ryan in "When Harry Met Sally." He's risking nothing except your reputation. He's going to ruin you, and if he doesn't, she will. I don't want my mentee to be the first one to go. You're smart and you're good and Justin is fucking you literally and figuratively. End it.

[*Beat.*]

Then this is the last time that I'm meeting with you. You are officially no longer my mentee. I can't work with people who make stupid choices. How do you think I made partner before 40? I fucking killed myself for 10 years. I came in at the end of the Taking-Clients-Out-For-Sexist-Activities era that led to the Endless-Diversity-Workshop era which pissed off all the older partners. There was one female partner who never lifted a finger to help me. All she did was tell me not to have kids on the one day we were alone in the elevator. A year later, she was out. I couldn't "lean in" since there was no one to lean in to. I have done my best to help you climb the ladder, but if you are going to do something as idiotic as sleep with your boss, then I can't be associated with you anymore.

SHERLOCK HOLMES AND THE ADVENTURE OF THE ELUSIVE EAR
David MacGregor

Dramatic
MARIE CHARTIER, late 20s–30s

MARIE CHARTIER, *daughter of the late Professor Moriarty, reveals her plans to corner the Postimpressionist art market to Sherlock Holmes.*

MARIE My game, as you call it, is a very deep one, Mr. Holmes. Being a criminal mastermind is difficult enough. Do you have any idea how hard it is being a female criminal mastermind? As you so perceptively observed, I am brilliant, ruthless, and beautiful. Not only that, I am the daughter of the celebrated Professor Moriarty, but do you think anyone in the world of organized crime would give me the time of day? Pah! It is a glorified boys' club filled with greedy and ignorant men. Would they let me into the drug trade? No. Gambling? No. Steel, oil, finance? No. Every door was closed against me. And so at length, I resolved to carve my own path . . . into the world of art. Naturally, I went first to Paris, and made the acquaintance of Georges Seurat, Toulouse-Lautrec, and Paul Gauguin, all of them poor, largely unrecognized, with chaotic personal lives and assorted addictions, yet all of them utterly devoted to their art to an obsessive degree. Of course they are men, and like most men, easily manipulated by a heartless seductress like myself. I left each one of them reeling with hope and desire, then travelled to the south of France, to the little village of Arles, where Vincent Van Gogh became my pet project. I made certain that he sent only his weakest paintings to his brother Theo, while I kept the rest. As for the others, when any of their work raises a ripple of interest, I simply have my agents take it off the market. You see, the quality of their work is one thing, but it is, after all, merely smudges of color on canvas. So where is the value? The profit? I put it to you that it is not in the paintings themselves, rather it is their stories, their tortured, unhappy, miserable lives that will make their paintings almost priceless in the very near future because these painters possess precisely what upper-class, wealthy collectors want, the one thing they can't buy—an authentic life.

SING THE BODY ELECTRIC
Michael Hollinger

Seriocomic
CLAIRE, 30s-40s

CLAIRE *is in group therapy. It's her turn to talk. She has a bandage over one eye.*

CLAIRE   Sometimes I feel like I've spent my whole life in the dark. I mean about love and sex. Bumpin' inta things, like a blind person; gettin' hurt; makin' the same mistakes, *over* and *over* and *over* . . . I don't know what it is about me that seems to attract the assholes, pardon my French. I mean, is there like a neon sign above my head sayin' "Assholes Welcome"? 'Cause I don't know how else to explain it. They just *find* me.

[*Indicating her bandage.*]

See this? Seven stitches. I counted every one of 'em goin' in. This'll leave a scar for damn sure, and maybe that's not such a bad thing, when all's said and done. To have a reminder, right on your body, to keep you from slidin' down that same old slippery slope. Like one a them warnin' lights on your dashboard? Though, to be perfectly honest, I tend to ignore them, too . . . 'Cause love and sex, they mark us, whether we like it or not. Inside and out. I guess all I got left to say is: I am *done* with this love and sex thing. I mean for good. I can deal with the inside scars; maybe that's just the price of admission. But once they start showin' up on your body . . . like when your eyebrow winds up on the receivin' end of some guy's class ring? That's when you say, "*Enough* a this *goddamn, fuckin' bullshit.*"

[*Beat. She strokes her bandage.*]

Pardon my French.

STRING

Jessica Lind Peterson

Dramatic
JOY, 33

JOY is speaking to her husband, CLIFF. *She has surprised* CLIFF *by flying to Cincinnati where he is attending an adhesive technology conference. Their marriage has lost its pizzazz and she has been questioning whether or not to leave him. An unexpected pregnancy quickly puts things into perspective.*

JOY I was just saying that I've been having kind of a hard time with us lately and I've been doing a lot of thinking about marriage and you and everything and I was kind of at a loss. I mean, I don't know if you've noticed that I've been slightly irritable this past month. Well, I don't know if irritable is the right word but I've been prone to random bursts of emotion and it mostly boils down to one thing. The thing about us not being the way we used to be. And at first I thought that's what's supposed to happen to married couples. Like as time passes we slowly start being repulsed by each other. And I thought, maybe it's me. Maybe I'm just not as attractive as I used to be or maybe I'm not as funny or cute anymore because let's face it, thirty-three is getting up there I mean, I'm almost middle age. But the point is that I'm just not ready to deal with all of this right now, I mean, I have a career and everything to think about and I want to feel important and attractive but I haven't been because of what's been hap-pening with us. But the major point here is that I've been trying to make a decision about what to do about this and the thought of us not being together anymore entered my head. I don't know. I'm not sure. I mean, I did think about it a little. I'm only saying the thought crossed my mind and for a split second the thought of being on my own again seemed very appealing. But please Cliff, the point I'm trying to get at here is that something happened and kind of put it all into perspective. The whole being attracted to each other thing is an important thing but I'm willing to overlook it for now and try and work on it but I don't know if we're going to have much time to work on it because pretty soon I'm going to be fat and ugly and there is no way you are going to be attracted to a big fat pregnant girl. [*Beat.*] I'm pregnant, Cliff.

STRING

Jessica Lind Peterson

Dramatic
RAINA, early 30s

RAINA *is speaking to* RYAN. RAINA *has just left her boyfriend,*
DEREK, *and is at the train station when she runs in to* RYAN. RYAN,
*a lawn care entrepreneur who delivers pizzas on the side, has been
trying to woo* RAINA *but has been unable to compete with* DEREK, *a
handsome professor of medieval literature. In this moment,* RAINA
confesses that RYAN *reminds her of her late father, and finally opens
up about her fear of falling in love.*

RAINA It's because of you, okay? This way that you are, you're
so . . . And I am pissed at you because none of this was in the
plan and you just keep showing up everywhere like Dobby
the Elf! Train stations, and dreams and Kitty Clinics. Enough
already! You think you love me right now, you think you actually know me enough to love me? Did it ever occur to you
that I actually might be boring? Did you ever think of that?
Maybe I'm just a girl who likes poetry and hates wearing
socks, okay? And we'll go on two actual dates and you'll figure out that I'm not the girl of your dreams, that I look really
weird without mascara on, that I'm actually an *idiot* because
I almost moved in with a guy I thought I loved and I don't
know why I thought that, maybe because he's tall and wears
corduroy blazers, and my god I almost *got rid of my cat* and
I'm not Elizabeth and you're not Robert Browning.

[*Beat.*]

He was just like you. God, if you could have seen him. He was
weird and he was wild and he had this overwhelming pas-
sion that just oozed out of him and stuck to you. He planted
this huge rose garden for my mom. I mean, our entire yard

was filled with roses. And he put a big stump right in the middle of it and he would sit there on that stump and play his guitar and annoy the neighbors and my mom would shush him through the kitchen window, but eventually she would give in and come out and sit with him and he would make up stupid songs about her and they would laugh.

[*Beat.*]

And then he died. And when he died my mom stopped laughing and her face started sinking. She became an old lady right in front of me. Now the yard is one big tangle of weeds. And I'm scared, Ryan. I'm so scared of all of it. I want to be in love like that but what if it stops one day?

SYCORAX: CYBER QUEEN OF QAMARA
Fengar Gael

Seriocomic
SYCORAX, age 500 years

SYCORAX, *the exiled Algerian sorceress and mother of* CALIBAN *(from Shakespeare's* The Tempest*), speaks to the audience. In the original production, she sent this out via live streaming.*

SYCORAX I, Sycorax, command your attention! Harken to my live streaming sorcery! This hag's voice and visage appearing on your own and every functioning screen in the electrified world, is mine! Yes, I, Sycorax, mother of Caliban, mistress of Ariel, am still among you, hacking into your wretched lives and the lives of your misguided governments. My mission began when a Duke of Milan named Prospero slandered my name, but I've been patient: while Big Brother was watching, Big Sister was waiting! Waiting five centuries to tell my side of the story; five hundred years for the wicked web of the Internet to bestow the widest possible audience in every dialect in every language on every continent, so the French hear me speaking French, the Chinese hear me speaking Mandarin, the South Americans hear Spanish, the North Americans hear English, and so forth. For sorcerers, the past can be regained as well as retained, so behold the truth of my tale told by my family of avatars, equipped with digitized, downloaded memories which were culled, scanned, and preserved to hold as much data as twelve sixty-four gigabyte smartphones. They know their names, their lineage, the history of everything quantifiable from their limited times and cultures; plus they possess extensive vocabularies, recognize indigenous plants and animals; they can farm, cook, sing, dance, masticate, defecate, fly a plane, and mix a martini, ha, ha! But before I introduce them, let me give you some background information missing from Wikipedia and the World Wide Web of lies, lies, and more lies! Yes, I want you to know that I have not been wasting my time. Thanks to the pagan god, Setebos, I was allowed to render myself invisible, but as the years passed, I felt increasingly restless, so I started doing the sort of things invisible witches do—and I don't mean hat tricks, ha, ha! At first, I was content with tipping teapots, hiding latchkeys; then I progressed to buckling carpets, toppling ladders, yanking canes. Later I advanced to spooking horses, starting fires, thinning ice, breaking wheels on carts and nudging surgeons' elbows—oh, that was great fun! Then later, much later, I tinkered with the brakes of buses, pushed buttons on the control panels of planes, trains, and street lights causing so many wrecks, I lost count, ha, ha! Naturally, I had great sport with guns, placing loaded pistols near homicidal boys, and of course with computers, mischief is easier than ever: all the fingers I prodded towards "send"; all the compromising pictures snapped; the hard drives destroyed, some containing the seminal work of poets, scientists, academics. Oh, the demotions, divorces, and suicides—you've no idea! You may think revenge was sweet and yes, it brought some relief, but I never quite achieved the catharsis I craved. I never felt a sense of restored harmony since I never regained what I'd lost: my reputation. Thanks to Prospero, I was aligned in a frivolous farce for the whole world to witness year after year, century after century! So it's time the world heard the truth! My avatars will prove that I, Sycorax, was not a "foul" but fair witch and doting mother; Caliban was not a brute; Ariel was not a slave; and the island of Qamara was mine, my kingdom before your countrymen colonized and destroyed it!

THREE MILES OF BAD ROAD
Rhea MacCallum

Dramatic
CANDACE, mid-20s and up

CANDACE *begs for her sister's time and attention while in the desert on a late-night hunt for signs of alien life.*

CANDACE   You really can't stand spending time with me, can you? You hate me, you're miserable and you're counting down the seconds until I give up on trying to bond with you so you can go back to your husband and your boys and go back to ignoring my existence. You didn't even want to come on this trip with me. This vacation of ours that was supposed to be a girls trip, supposed to be just you and me, only you couldn't do that. You had to bring your whole brood along and did I complain? No. I adjusted my expectations because that's what I do but I still thought maybe we could create an experience together. Is that really asking for too much? I mean, really, what do I have to do to make you want to spend time with me? That's all I want. A little bit of your time. A few moments every once in a while, checking in with each other. It would be nice if you were the one to call me sometimes, just to talk, no agenda, no calendared event, birthday party, holiday event to figure out, but just because. We used to talk all the time. And get our hair done together and go to the movies and grab lunch and spend hours in the card aisle at the grocery store making fun of all the saccharine sentiments and we'd laugh until we were crying and hunched over with stomach aches. I realize we're not in that place anymore and that's fine, lives evolve, but I thought, just maybe this alien hunt thing would be an adventure, a bonding experience. A little time in the desert, a few laughs while indulging in the fanciful notion that there's something out here worth searching for. I don't actually expect us to find proof of alien life tonight but I thought we might, I don't know, rediscover our friendship. I miss my sister. But if spending time with me is so awful then maybe you should go back to the hotel. I can look for the damn aliens by myself.

THREE MORE SISTERS
Christi Stewart-Brown

Comic
JAN, early to mid-20s

Three More Sisters *can best be described as a mash-up theatrical piece about famous sets of three sisters from history, music, television, movies, literature, and stage plays. This monologue features* JAN *as* MEG *from* Crimes of the Heart, *written by the author.*

JAN (*as* MEG)   A lot of families have three girls for the following reasons: a couple gets married, they plan on having two children, a boy and a girl. One boy, one girl, that's all. Preferably the boy should be older. So the couple has a girl first. Dad starts to sweat, but better luck next time. Maybe. The couple has a second girl. Dad is deeply disappointed. Mom feels like a failure. This second girl is the source of the distress. This second girl will have trouble all her life because she will be the middle child because they were so disappointed that she was a girl that they will, of course, decide to try one more time even though they can't afford a third child, but they have one anyway because they WANT THAT BOY! It's a girl, Mr. Magrath. Mr. Magrath, I regret to inform you that your third child is a girl. But instead of being disappointed that the third child is a girl, Dad is still mad at the second child for being a girl. After all, if she had been a boy, they wouldn't have had to have a third child. It never really matters what the third child is—who could blame her for being a girl? She didn't know they were hoping for a boy. The second girl, she's the problem, she should have known, she should have known that she should have been a boy. Mom and Dad gave up after that—no more children, certainly no more *girls*. The youngest was dad's favorite, of course. Dad felt she was innocent of all wrong-doing, unlike the first two, one of whom should have been a boy. Nevertheless, the sister who was given the right, the okay, the go ahead, to be a girl—was named Bob. Junior. Robert Magrath, Junior. Not Roberta. Robert. Bob. Bobby. We just call her Baby.

THREE MORE SISTERS
Christi Stewart-Brown

Seriocomic
OLGA, early to mid-20s

Three More Sisters *can best be described as a mash-up theatrical piece about famous sets of three sisters from history, music, television, movies, literature, and stage plays. This monologue was written by the author for OLGA from Chekhov's* The Three Sisters.

OLGA   I had a date last week with an upstanding young man, a bit older than I—more sophisticated. We'd had a lovely evening, I was flushed from the excitement. We went to a concert and then for a walk in the park. When he brought me home, there was no one awake and we sat in the parlor by ourselves talking. I felt as though I could have talked all night with Boris, so similar were our minds. But then—-then he leant over and kissed me. I felt the color rise to my cheek. I smiled. He kissed me again. And I—I—dare I say it? I kissed him back! Hesitantly at first. But he pressed his lips to mine with increasing fervour and I, in turn, returned his ardent kisses, for truly it excited in me feelings which I had never before experienced. I wanted him to continue, which he did. And then, oh dear—then his hand, which had heretofore rested on the back of the sofa, gently slid along my bodice, stroking the silky fabric and all that lay beneath its surface. My cheeks burned like fire—I felt alive—I felt as if we were of one mind, each answering the other need for need. I felt him begin to loosen the laces of my bodice and my body leapt with pleasure. But, alas, a vision rose before me—a vision of the fires of hell enveloping me for my fleshly weakness—a vision which utterly quenched the flames that were coming from within me. And so I gently pushed poor Boris away. He needed no explanation. He smiled at me tenderly. "It is good that you have stopped me, little Olga," he said, "for if you had allowed me to continue, I would have known that you were not worthy of my love." Not worthy! I did not understand. "Olya," he continued, "I know now that you are of a respectable nature, a woman of principles who would not allow a man to take too many liberties—these are qualities that men will seek when looking for a wife." He left me then. I felt so ashamed. Ashamed because I did not want him to stop.

TOURISTS OF THE MINDFIELD
Glenn Alterman

Seriocomic
ALICE, 30s–40s

ALICE, a small-town librarian, has secretly been in love with BOB since high school, but he's never given her a second look. Naturally she's shocked and delighted when out of the blue, he asks her out on a date. They are sitting in his car right in front of her house.

ALICE   It's all like predetermined, pre-ordained, whatever you want to call it, Bob. Everyone knows it, ya learn it in Life 101. There are no accidents, no, none! Not even here, in small town U.S.A. We all bump, melt, merge, whatever you want to call it, with people we are meant to meet, MEANT-TO-MEET! I believe that, I do. I mean think about it, just think about it Bob, fact that you're here, I'm here, and we're both sitting in your car, front of my house, ready to go, night on the town, no accident, no-none. No mistake. Preordained. And I want you to know, want you to know Bob, I was *thrilled* when you called last week. Thought oh my God, BOB, imagine, finally! After all these years! Not that I was sitting by the phone, no. I'm so busy these days at the library, non-stop, books back and forth; library lunacy. So you were lucky to even get me in. Lucky I was home. Luck, lucky, pre-ordained. But it was certainly a surprise. I mean after all these years of seeing you at the supermarket, passing you on the street, seeing you drive by. Certainly a surprise. And now, here, the two of us, sitting in your car,

[A forced smile.]

waiting . . . waiting patiently, may I add, for you put the key in the ignition so we can go somewhere and . . . . So why don't you start the car, Bob? Car can't start by itself. You don't want me to leave, do you? I can't go. Not now, Bob, you don't understand. This is . . . This is a brand new dress! Just got it. And this is our first . . . You don't understand. Bob, Bobby, ROBERT! This has all been pre-ordained!

THE TRUE
Sharr White

Dramatic
DOROTHEA, late 50s

DOROTHEA *is a behind-the-scenes political operative who has worked to keep* ERASTUS, *the mayor of a large city in upstate New York, in office for decades. He has barely survived a primary challenge. Here, she chastises him, and by extension the whole local Democratic Party, for complacency.*

DOROTHEA   What a humiliation. Even *Peter* knows how close Touhey came. Thirty-five hundred votes! A Republican! In a Democratic town! And at the same time as lyin' cocksucker Nixon's on teevee lyin' his cock off about cocksucking Watergate! 'Rastus, the whole organization's slipping. Used to be, a, a . . . a man gets crippled on the job, say? Or God forbid, dies? Whatever? Say, leaves a mother with three children? By God that funeral would get paid for. Committeeman would come by the house next day, that mother would have a job. And you know who would get the vote next fall? Democrats! For thirty-five years, people would say *Dan O'Connell* in one breath, *Erastus Corning* with the next. You as Mayor, him as Party Chairman. I didn't want to bring any of this up, thought you could see it *yourself,* but maybe you can't. *Regular* people. They don't give a shit what you do behind closed doors so long as their lives are working. But their lives aren't working any more. Committeeman. Used to know every. Single. Voter. In his district. Every single one. That voter had a problem, they told the committeeman, the committeeman went to the Ward leader, the Ward leader either solved it? Or went to Dan. And you know what happened at the end of the day? It got taken care of. *Now* all people can see is committeemen with no-show city contracts who don't even care what their name is. Look at Ward 3. Okay? You're losing Third Ward. Why's that? The blacks. Because who aren't they related to? The Irish! A Ward 3 mother's got a problem? Kid with potential, some kid the committeeman should *know*— let's say the kid gets hassled by a cop, lands some trumped-up charges to teach 'im a lesson, that Ward 3 mother doesn't have anybody to turn to, because whoever the fuck—*Hurkus McGurkis*—doesn't bother to know the people in his Ward because, well, thirty years ago it was Irish and all he knows is Irish people, of which there are maybe fifteen left in all of Ward 3, and he won't get to know any blacks. Well whose fault is that? Thirty years ago, Ward leader would show up, walk the kid out of the station house and see him home. But not now; this black kid is fuckin' fucked. And that Ward 3 mother? Who's *she* voting for? Let me tell you who. Nobody fuckin' knows. When we were all doing our job, Erastus, we knew what she was having for *dinner*. You know why? Because we were eating it *with* her.

UNTIL THE SKIES CLEAR
Merridith Allen

Dramatic
CASSIE, 30s

CASSIE, *who recently lost her baby at five days old, explains the unimaginable grief she feels to her twin sister,* VIOLET.

CASSIE   DO I SEEM FINE TO YOU?

[*Silence.*]

> I started the tattoos when my husband started sleeping with that girl—the ah—how old was she, 18, maybe. I would tattoo things on my body—things I've lost. The first one sucked, but then it was like a high. Something would hurt me, I'd get a tattoo, let the wound heal, and then I would feel better. Always black ink. No color, that was important to me. I didn't want any color. My first baby—Rob named her Laura. You didn't know, but, she was still-born. She's right here. And then Daddy, right here. Mom. Aunt Elizabeth. Marmalade—that cat I loved down the street. I was thinking, I'd tattoo Adam's right here.

[*She indicates a spot on her chest.*]

> Close to my heart. But then I thought, no, not this time. It's not going to be enough, this time. [*Pause.*] Loss is like . . . someone's fist, squeezing your guts. It hurts, but you can do things about it. I can always find ways to cope—ways to get myself up in the morning. Losing Adam . . . the loss is not the thing that is impossible. What's impossible is that, I can look around, and everything else is the same. People get up, they go to work. Somewhere, some woman is cooking dinner for her family, making love to her husband—and you know something? That woman—that apparition in my mind—she looks like me. Some phantom version of myself who knows

what being happy is—who doesn't take a bit of food and think her baby can't. Who doesn't drink, and think—oh, right, I'm not pregnant, who doesn't think about sex and think about the kind of love it took to make that tiny person, with a heartbeat like a hummingbird, and big blue eyes and peach-colored skin. The fact that the world turns, and Adam is gone, and Laura is gone, and my husband is gone, and . . . being broken hearted—that doesn't even do it. It feels like I have no heart—there is a fucking chasm right here where my heart is supposed to be. And right outside that door, there are children laughing and people falling in love, and it is IMPOSSIBLE for me to make sense of any of it. That is now I am, instead of *fine*. And you're not fine either.

WE THE SISTERS
Laura Neill

Dramatic
BECKY, 30s

BECKY *is in the office of a sorority sister,* LARA, *who is now a conservative US congresswoman.* BECKY *has come to plead with her to vote no on yet another bill to repeal Obamacare and replace it with a new law that will gut people's healthcare coverage. Predictably,* LARA *supports this bill and doesn't care what it will do to people's coverage. But* BECKY *has an ace up her sleeve.*

BECKY   I think you do remember, Congresswoman. I think you remember very clearly how I helped you copy-and-paste your final paper for your senior English seminar. I think you remember very, very clearly how you were in tears because your thesis advisor had told you you were getting a B and losing Phi Beta Kappa and how you were in the 1902 room shoveling peanut butter cookies into your face moaning that your life was fucking over and how could you go on and how you begged me, begged me, ON YOUR KNEES BEGGED ME to bring you a fucking Four Loko and some weed because you wanted to get real high and forget all your problems. And I think you remember how instead of getting you wasted, I sat you down and googled with you until we found a nice-looking old dissertation from the University of Michigan and I typed it all out for you, Congresswoman. I'm pretty sure you remember all that, that I held your hand for a minute and then got on typing that whole paper out for you like it was your own, while you sniffled and thanked me over and over for being the best Thetalover in the whole damn house. And I'm very, very sure you remember sending that in to your professor at two thirty-six a.m. and holding your breath for the next fourteen days until graduation praying that no one would put it through Turn It In, and getting real drunk with me graduation morning when you realized they hadn't. When you realized you'd gotten away with it. When you realized you had graduated Dartmouth College on a lie ... I'm absolutely certain you remember all that. Because you might have your hand on that panic button but you haven't pressed it yet.

WE THE SISTERS

Laura Neill

Dramatic
LARA, 30s

LARA *is a conservative US congresswoman about to vote for a bill that will gut Obamacare. BECKY, a sorority sister, has come to her office to please with her to vote no. When LARA will not budge, BECKY has threatened to blackmail her by telling the world that she helped LARA graduate from Dartmouth by plagiarizing a paper. LARA has offered BECKY a check for a large sum of money to help defray her mother's medical bills. BECKY won't take the check.*

LARA   You fucking idiot. If you can't see that this is your mother's only chance—you fucking child. We're not in college anymore, Becky, we're not in the land of throwing drinks on each other when we disagree. We are not in the land of Keystone Light and senior year and setting off the fire alarm at three in the morning with our fucking popcorn and Buffy the Vampire Slayer, we are not the EZT. We are adults now. And look at the kind of adults we are. *You* are a yoga coach who can't make enough money to buy her mother's medicine. *I* am the future first female president of the United States of America. You are the rest and I am the best. And when I offer you something you take it. Grow up, Becky. You're gonna let your little games cause your mother pain? Because if you don't take this check, Becky, that's what you're doing. You're causing your mother pain. You can throw sixty-dollar scotch in my face and storm out of my office all you want, but her pain tolerance is just gonna get lower . . . and lower . . . and lower . . . and Scalise-Abraham is gonna pass. If not tomorrow, then soon. You think your mother cares about my college essay? You think she cares how you get her medicine? I think she cares about her pain. Because she is *in pain. Your* *mother is in pain.* You've spent your entire life being a terrible fucking disappointment, saddling your mother with your college debt, dropping out of law school, shattering all the hopes she had for you one by one . . . Are you really going to disappoint her again? You better think really hard before you walk out that door. Because if you're going to be a child, you sure as hell better be a good one.

WE WILL NOT BE SILENT
David Meyers

Dramatic
SOPHIE, 21

We Will Not Be Silent *tells the true story of* SOPHIE SCHOLL, *a German college student who led the only major act of civil disobedience against the Nazis during World War II. During the course of the play,* SOPHIE's *interrogator promises to save her life if she will confess and renounce her actions. Although* SOPHIE *struggles with the decision, she ultimately decides that she cannot compromise herself and her beliefs in order to save her life. But on the morning of her trial and execution, the impact of* SOPHIE's *decision finally weighs on her. As she waits in her prison cell with her brother* HANS, SOPHIE *desperately seeks a way out.*

SOPHIE   No. I can't, Hans. I can't. I don't want to die. I want to live. I want to wake up tomorrow, and the next day. I want to marry Fritz and be a mother. To read books, and play music—to pick berries, and see the trees. Help me, please. Tell them—tell them that I—

[*She calls out to the guards.*]

I'll sign it! Whatever you want. I'll say it—on the radio, in the papers. I don't want to die!

[*Back to Hans.*]

I want to be young and happy—to laugh, and draw, and write poems—beautiful, beautiful poems. I want to go along—like everyone else. To ignore what is happening. There is nothing after this—it all just ends. We won't be remembered . . . Why couldn't we just accept that? That we're not special. That none of this matters. I want to open my eyes, and see the Spring—the violets, the orchids. I want to taste chocolate, and butter, and sausage. To see Mama, and

Papa. To grow old, and sick—and be glad it rained . . . I want to run through the forest and give cocoa to my children. I can't die. I can't.

[*She calls out to the guards again.*]

I'll say it! I'll confess—to everything. Please. I don't want to die. Don't let them kill me. Please!

WITH LOVE AND A MAJOR ORGAN
Julia Lederer

Dramatic
ANABEL, 20s–30s

ANABEL *is speaking to us, at the beginning of the play, trying to understand how she feels.*

ANABEL   My heart has started beating so loudly that some-times I wonder if other people can hear it. Louder than their audio books, their music, their spinning brains. My heart. Beating away. Like I'm a busker playing my feelings on the subway platform, in a movie theatre, in my cubicle at work. Heart strings. So, I went to see a therapist. I asked her to listen to my heart. She said that she wasn't allowed to touch me. It crossed the boundaries of our relationship. I asked her to define "boundaries." She asked me about my mother. I said, "I don't think my heart issue is hereditary." She said, "All issues are somewhat hereditary. Now tell me about your mother. Remember, I have a degree." [*Pause.*] My mother. My mother told me her heart was like a ball of yarn. That it would get caught on other people—on a backpack zipper, a large hoop earring, one of those buttons that reads "VOTE." They wouldn't realize her attachment, and they'd move further and further away. The more the distance that grew between them, the more she'd unravel. More and more yarn got snagged, pulled out, until she was tangled everywhere. Her feelings in knots all over town. She said it was humiliat-ing. I thought it sounded sort of pretty. Public art. And my therapist said "Hmmmm." But in a profound way. Like some-one who has a degree. So, I kept talking. About how I feel ev-erything. About how I want to put my ear to people's chests. Instead of a sweaty handshake. Instead of half-hearted wave. Or a text. Of a heart shaped emoji, not even anatomically accurate. Not accurate at all. And. And, if you can't know anyone else, then you're always alone. A snail with a shell that looks like a rock. Armored and camouflaged. Often eaten in places as a delicacy. My therapist took a deep breath. She scratched her nose. She said, "Some people have high emotional toxicity." By "some people" she obviously meant me. (I also have a degree.) Toxic emotions. I don't know if this is a danger or a super power. I don't know if what's inside me is harsh or beautiful. I didn't ask her opinion. But I don't want a ball of yarn or a toxic leak in my chest. That's not what this is. I think it's—My heart is like a lantern.

RIGHTS AND PERMISSIONS

ACCORDING TO THE CHORUS © 2019 by Arleen Hutton. Reprinted by permission of the author . For performance rights, contact Arleen Hutton, betharlene@me.com.

AFTER © 2019 by Michael McKeever. Reprinted by permission of Barbara Hogenson, Barbara Hogenson Agency. For performance rights, contact Barbara Hogenson, bhogenson@aol.com.

THE AFTERPARTY © 2018 by Reina Hardy. Reprinted by permission of Susan Gurman, Gurman Agency. For performance rights, contact Susan Gurman, susan@gurmanagency.com.

AMERICA ADJACENT © 2019 by Boni B. Alvarez. Reprinted by permission of the author. For performance rights, contact Boni B. Alvarez, boni.b.alvarez@gmail.com.

AMERICAN SON © 2015 by Christopher Demos-Brown. Reprinted by permission of Ali Tesluk Samuel French, Inc. For performance rights, Samuel French, Inc., 212-206-8990, www.samuelfrench.com.

THE ANTELOPE PARTY © 2018 by Eric John Mayer. Reprinted by permission of the author. For performance rights, contact Broadway Play Publishing, 212-772-8334, www.broadwayplaypubl.com.

ANYWHERE © 2019 by Michael Ross Albert. Reprinted by permission of Colin Rivers, Marquis Entertainment, Inc.. For performance rights, contact Michael Ross Albert, crivers@marquisent.ca.

APES AT PLAY © 2019 by Jonathan Yukich. Reprinted by permission of the author. For performance rights, contact Jonathan Yukich, yukich5@gmail.com.

BABEL © 2019 by Jacquelyn Goldfinger. Reprinted by permission of Amy Wagner, Abrams Artist Agency. For performance rights, please contact Amy Wagner, amy.wagner@abramsartny.com.

BAILEY'S COLLEGE FUND © 2019 by James Hindman. Reprinted by permission of the author. For performance rights, contact James Hindman, seidojim@aol.com.

THE BANANA WAR © 2007 by Arnold Johnston & Deborah Percy. Reprinted by permission of thre authors. For performance rights, contact Arnold Johnston & Deborah Percy, arnie.johnston@wmich.edu.

BERNHARDT/HAMLET © 2018 by Madwoman in the Attic, Inc. Reprinted by permission of Amy Mellman, ICM Partners. For performance rights, contact Samuel French, Inc., 212-206-8990, www.samuelfrench.com.

BIG SCARY ANIMALS © 2018 by Matt Lyle. Reprinted by permission of the author. For performance rights, contact Matt Lyle, mattdlyle77@gmail.com.

BIRDS OF A FEATHER; A Comedy About De-Extunction © 2019 by June Guralnick. Reprinted by permission of the author. For performance rights, contact June Guralnick, juneguralnik@gmail.com.

BOMBER'S MOON © 2019 by Deborah Yarchun. Reprinted by permission of the author. For performance rights, contact Deborah Yarchun, deborah.yarchun@gmail.com.

BOTTICELLI VENUS © 2017 by Don Nigro. Reprinted by permission of the author. For performance rights, contact Samuel French, Inc., 212-206-8990, www.samuelfrench.com.

A BRIEF HISTORY OF PENGUINS AND PROMISCUITY © 2017 by James McLindon. Reprinted by permission of the author. For performance rights, contact James McLindon, jimmclindon@gmail.com.

BUMP © 2018 by Chiara Atik. Reprinted by permission of the author. For performance rights, contact Dramatists Play Service, 440 Park Ave. S., New York, NY 10016, (www.dramatists.com) (212-683-8960).

CATCH THE BUTCHER © 2018 by Adam Seidel. Reprinted by permission of the author. For performance rights, contact Adam Seidel, seidel54@gmail.com.

CHELSEA PERKINS © 2019 by Aren Haun. Reprinted by permission of the author. For performance rights, contact Aren Haun, arenhaun@gmail.com.

CLARTÉ © 2019 by Lavinia Roberts. Reprinted by permission of the author. For performance rights, contact Lavinia Roberts, laviniaroberts@yahoo.com.

COMBAT READY © 2016 by Laura Hirschberg. Reprinted by permission of the author. For performance rights, contact Laura Hirschberg, laura.hirschberg@gmail.com.

CONFEDERATES © 2019 by Suzanne Bradbeer, c/o Gay Isaacs. Reprinted by permission of the author. For performance rights, contact Amy Wagner, Abrams Artists Agency, amy.wagner@abramsartny.com.

DAY OF THE DOG © 2019 by Daniel Damiano. Reprinted by permission of the author. For performance rights, contact Daniel Damiano, damiano_daniel@yahoo.com.

DEAD AND BURIED © 2018 by James McLindon. Reprinted by permission of Shelley Corcoran, Dramatic Publishing Co. For performance rights, contact Shelley Corcoran, scorcoran@dpcplays.com.

DEAD MOVEMENT © 2018 by John Patrick Bray. Reprinted by permission of the author. For performance rights, contact John Patrick Bray, johnpatrickbray@gmail.com.

GREAT ROLES FOR OLD ACTRESSES © 2018 by Andrew W. Heinze. Reprinted by permission of the author. For performance rights, contact Andrew W. Heinze, arheinze@gmail.com.

FINDING A PLACE IN THE WORLD © 2019 by Meghan Gambling. Reprinted by permission of the author. For performance rights, contact Meghan Gambling, meghan.gambling@gmail.com.

HAPPY HARLEY © 2019 by Meghan Gambling. Reprinted by permission of the author. For performance rights, contact Meghan Gambling, meghan.gambling@gmail.com.

HARDBALL © 2018 by Victoria Stewart. Reprinted by permission of the author. For performance rights, contact Broadway Play Publishing, 212-772-8334, www.broadwayplaypubl.com.

HERCULES DIDN'T WADE IN THE WATER © 2019 by Michael A. Jones. Reprinted by permission of the author. For performance rights, contact Michael A. Jones, harlemarts@gmail.com.

HICKORYDICKORY © 2014 Marisa Wegrzyn. Reprinted by permission of Chris Till, Creative Artists Agency. For performance rights, contact Broadway Play Publishing, 212-772-8334, www.broadwayplaypubl.com.

HORNY BASTARDS © 2018 by Sam Graber. Reprinted by permission of the author. For performance rights, contact Sam Graber, samgraber@outlook.com.

HUMAN RITES © 2018 by Seth Rozin. Reprinted by permission of Susan Gurman, Gurman Agency. For performance rights, contact Susan Gurman, susan@gurmanagency.com.

IDIO © 2017 by Abbey Fenbert. Reprinted by permission of the author. For performance rights, contact Abbey Fenbert, afenbert@gmail.com.

JUMP © 2019 by Elayne Heilveil. Reprinted by permission of the author. For performance rights, contact Elayne Heilveil, elaynerh@aol.com.

KIM KARDASHIAN PRESENTS MAXIM GORKY'S THE LOWER DEPTHS © 2019 by Daniel Damiano. Reprinted by permission of the author. For performance rights, contact Daniel Damiano, damiano_daniel@yahoo.com.

LAY ME DOWN © 2019 by Panny Jackson. Reprinted by permission of the author. For performance rights, contact Panny Jackson, pennybjackson@gmail.com.

LOVE AND OTHER EQUATIONS © 2019 by Merridith Allen. Reprinted by permission of the author. For performance rights, contact Merridith Allen, merridith.allen26@gmail.com.

MAKE MULCH FROM IT © 2017 by Arianna Rose. Reprinted by permission of the author. For performance rights, contact Arianna Rose, rockawayrose@gmail.com.